Old Man Abroad

Also by the Author

A Daddy's Advice: Volume 1 (2014)
A Daddy's Advice: Volume 2 (2015)
A Daddy's Advice: Volume 3 (2015)
A Daddy's Advice: Volume 4 (2017)
A Picture Story of Trekking and Surviving, Nepal 2015 (2015)
Trekking the Inca Trail to Machu Picchu, Peru 2016, (2016)

Old Man Abroad

Trading Rain for Blue Skies

Barry Torrens

Disclaimer

This book is a memoir based on the author's personal experiences and reflections. While every effort has been made to ensure accuracy, certain events, names and details may have been altered to respect the privacy of individuals or for narrative flow. The views and opinions expressed in this book are solely those of the author and do not represent those of any affiliated organisations or individuals.

The author and publisher disclaim any liability for any outcomes resulting from actions taken based on the contents of this book. Readers are encouraged to seek professional advice where appropriate.

I would like to dedicate this book to my wonderful children, Banana, Penster and Big Bad Bill. Remain positive, confident and play by your own rules.

About the Author

Barry Torrens is from the north coast of Northern Ireland. He is an ex-barrister, pilot and residential/commercial landlord. When his final child of his three children left for university in 2023, he decided there was nothing stopping him from fulfilling a dream of his, i.e. to live in Tuscany, so he sold/gave everything away and emigrated to Italy in August 2023. Barry set up an English school, the Toscana English Academy, in the local town where he lives, and he is successfully teaching Tuscans how to speak English. This is a memoir of his first 12 months living in Italy. You can follow how he is now settling into his new life by visiting his popular 'Old Man Abroad' page on TikTok, Facebook and Instagram.

Any spare time Barry gets, he enjoys adventure trekking, having climbed most of the highest mountains in the UK and Ireland, Gran Paradiso (Italy), Mont Blanc (France), Maccu Picchu (Peru) and Everest Base Camp (Nepal – where he and his sister survived the deadly earthquake of 2015).

Barry is passionate about Italy and Tuscany in particular. He first visited Italy over 30 years ago and returned many times over the years. He bought a property in Montaione in 2016 and moved there as a permanent resident in 2023.

If you follow his journey online, you will know that he is enjoying *La Dolce Vita* (the sweet life). He now wants to share his experience and hopes to inspire others to step out of their comfort zones.

Acknowledgements

First and foremost, I would like to thank my three wonderful children, Anna, Jennifer and William – or as I know them, Banana, Penster and Big Bad Bill. Without them I wouldn't have had a quarter of the life I currently enjoy. They are the centre of my world, and watching them grow into the beautiful young adults they are today has given me ten worlds of happiness. I have never seen my children argue amongst themselves, ever, and that is the greatest gift a father can have.

Thank you also to my sister Lesley not only for being a trusted companion but also for taking the time to sit and read and re-read drafts of this book. Lesley has been there in the great times, the good times and was still there during the rubbish times – thank you, Lego.

I would also like to thank Barbara, who edited this book, for her wisdom during this process. Her knowledge and precision are outstanding – as is her passion for Italy. I cannot recommend her highly enough. For editing work, visit her website at www.pensatostudios.com.

Thank you also to the people of Montaione for being patient, accepting, friendly and wonderful since my arrival. I know I am an outsider and still have to master the language, but their approach to me has been nothing short of amazing.

Any inaccuracies within this book are my own and belong entirely to me.

Barry Torrens

Contents

Chapter 1
The Decision

The wind and rain were so strong that the water droplets were being blown up my nose. It was the height of summer, and I was standing on the promenade in my hometown on my 53rd birthday, the 6th of July 2023. This scene cemented the start of a journey I had been contemplating for some time … 'Do it, Barry.'

An 'empty-nester', as defined in the dictionary, is someone whose children have grown up and left home. This phase of life, often viewed through a lens of melancholy, unexpectedly opened the door to a new world of opportunities for me. The imminent departure of my youngest to university marked not just the end of an era but the commencement of a personal renaissance.

For decades, my identity was that of a parent, a protector, an entertainer, a disciplinarian, an adviser and a provider. Now, the quietness of the house, once filled with chaos, echoed with memories and the ticking of a clock. It was a bittersweet memory of past laughter and the silent anticipation of the unknown. Yet, in this silence, I found a voice urging me to redefine my existence beyond the familiar roles I had played … 'Now, what do you want to do?'

The decision to become more than just an empty-nester wasn't an escape; it was an embrace of life's transitions. My journey up to this point had been an eclectic mix of experiences. I had scaled mountains, navigated the complex world of business, flown planes, welded oil rigs, practised law and even dabbled in politics. Each role I had taken on taught me something valuable – primarily the art of resilience and adaptability.

My reflections led me to a crossroads. The comfortable, predictable path demanded I stay, to continue in the predictable familiarity of my home, my community and my country. But comfort often breeds complacency and boredom, and I yearned for something that would reignite the spark of adventure in me.

The idea of relocating and starting again was not just a fleeting thought; it was a clear call for adventure. My mind wandered to Italy, a country I had fallen in love with during many visits since the first in 1994. The allure of its landscapes, the richness of its culture, the quality of its food and the warmth of its people had left an indelible mark on my heart. It was in Italy, particularly Tuscany, where I saw my next chapter unfolding … 'Could I? Should I?'

Problem number one in the planning phase: if I go, how will I pay the bills? For this venture I wanted to stick to what I knew – more or less. I knew learning Italian was going to be a difficult enough task at my age, never mind throwing in re-training to do another job, so I started thinking about what I knew and developed an idea from that. I knew English, how to speak it and how to write it – most Italians don't, not in rural Tuscany anyway. I researched Teaching English as a Foreign Language (TEFL) and that started me on a path of taking and passing courses to get qualified to teach, pre-departure. Teaching English in a land where it wasn't my native tongue presented an exciting challenge. My lifelong experience with the language, combined with a solid educational background and a few certificates, made me feel more than qualified for this task.

Planning this journey required a meticulous approach. I had to tell friends and family of my decision, which was met with a mixture of surprise and admiration, strangely and funnily not one 'don't go', but I'm hoping that was more down to the fact that they knew I had a pool and a spare bedroom.

As I started into the logistics, I realised the enormity of what I was undertaking. I was not just moving to a new country; I was about to immerse myself in a completely different way of life. The challenges were daunting, but the excitement of the adventure into the unknown pushed me forward.

The transition from being a full-time parent in UK and Ireland to an entrepreneur in Italy was a journey filled with emotions. I grappled with the reality of leaving behind a life that I had known for decades. There was a sense of loss for the familiar routines and the comfort of home. Yet there was also an exhilarating sense of freedom and a thrill at the thought of embracing a new beginning.

As I prepared for my departure, I found myself reflecting on my journey as a parent. The joys and challenges of raising three children had been the most rewarding part of my life. As they embarked on their own paths, I felt a deep sense of pride and love for them and a strong confidence in their abilities to navigate the world. Here's something I'm very proud of – and please bear with me for this self-indulgence. The children's mum and I always fostered closeness with the children. Their close age-group was planned, and I ensured they slept in the same bedroom as young children even though we had enough rooms for them to have one each. Each corner of their bedroom was decorated with either princesses or racing cars, depending on where they slept. And it worked: in all the years of their childhood and teenage lives, I never ever heard them argue between themselves, not once. I even had a neighbour come to my house to complain that, when in the garden, my children laughed too much, and it was disturbing him. Their mum and I had done a fabulous job. Now over to you, children. Find your lives, but remember we're always here, 24/7, 365.

The decision to move was solely mine. At the time of making the decision I was engaged to be married. The special person in my life, someone I had hoped would join me on this adventure, decided that she did not want to move from her town and live in Italy. She chose a different path. While I respected the decision, it added a layer of complexity to my emotions. She had a young son, and the decision could only be hers. Nevertheless, I was determined to embark on this journey, fortified by the love and support of my family and friends cheering me on from the sidelines ... 'Go, Barry – how big is your pool?', 'Go, Barry – can your spare room sleep six?'

A number of months before I decided to leave Northern Irish shores, I came up with an idea to start a sea shanty group. I had grown up in Portrush, a tourist seaside resort, so I was accustomed to the sea, but I hadn't the first clue how to sing or how to start a group of singers. So, I floated the idea online: 'Anyone fancy becoming part of a sea shanty group, the Causeway Shantymen, the Salty Seadogs?' I received many responses, but mostly from wives and girlfriends: 'For goodness' sake, please take my man and get him out of the house!'

A couple of Wednesdays later I had a group of 28 men, all keen and ready to sing some sea shanties at Portrush Yacht Club. They were and are an amazing bunch. We sang at weddings, at festivals, on Rathlin Island, on a tall ship, at the Riverside Theatre, at charity events and more. And they know how to party. I was so proud of them, and it was an honour and a pleasure being their captain. The only regret I had when leaving for Italy some six months later was that I left these Salty Seadogs behind. I left the group in the (more capable than me) hands of Captain Chris. They gave me a rousing send-off that would have brought a tear to Long John Silver's glass eye and promoted me to Commodore and Honorary President – which I think only means I have to buy the beers when there. I watch them from afar with a tinge of regret and pride. When I see them online, Captain Chris no doubt despairs at the ping on his phone when I ask 'Why is George not wearing his Seadogs' necktie?'.

This book, a chronicle of my journey from an Irish empty-nester to an English teacher in Italy, is more than just a memoir. It is a message of hope, a demonstration of the enduring spirit of adventure and a reminder that it's never too late to reinvent yourself. My story is one of transformation, of stepping out of my comfort zone and embracing the unknown with open arms. Will it work? As yet, I don't know, but it won't fail for the lack of effort.

Join me on this journey, not just as a passive observer but as an active participant in your own story of change and discovery. Let this book be a catalyst for you to explore new horizons, awaken your dormant passions and embrace the adventures that life offers. As we venture together into the heart of beautiful Tuscany and beyond, let's celebrate new beginnings, the joy of learning and the endless possibilities that await when we dare to dream and act. Welcome to Tuscany.

Chapter 2
Starting Out

Before crossing the half-century mark, my CV read like a rollercoaster ride, from piloting to air traffic control, welding on oil rigs, donning the wig of a barrister-at-law, and playing the roles of landlord and multiple business owner. Breaking free from limits has been a fundamental lesson in my life, shaping me into the man I am today. This book is about positivity, celebrating all things good and merry that bring a genuine smile to people's faces, hopefully. It's a rallying call to adventure and happiness, an anthem for maintaining a positive and optimistic outlook. In a world constantly trying to bring us down, it's about uplifting people, their moods, their spirits and their perceptions of this incredible world.

Don't get me wrong, I've had my fair share of sitting in that dark, gloomy corner more times than I'd like to admit. Yet I possessed the instincts, determination and strength to rise, turn and face the sun. In fact, that's one of the reasons I'm writing this book – to share an optimistic mindset and hopefully inspire others to do the same.

I was born on the 6th of July 1970. I was the youngest of five siblings. My parents, unable to remember if I arrived before or after midnight, settled for the 6th, giving me an excuse for two birthdays. Growing up in the tourist seaside town of Portrush, on the north coast of Northern Ireland, I had a childhood that was nothing short of wonderful, surrounded by loving parents, delightful siblings and a fun family atmosphere. Not everyone can say this, but I count myself lucky.

Even as a child, the seeds of adventure were firmly planted within me. Armed with nothing more than a bicycle, a wetsuit and a football, we created our own fun and had a fabulous time. Outdoor play and a developing sense of adventure defined my childhood. It would be almost impossible for children today to have such a childhood. It's all screens, screens, screens now. For three decades, my parents ran a beautiful guest house overlooking the sea. The sound of waves served as lullabies, and our days were filled with playing at the seaside – truly, a magnificent childhood.

Everything was perfect; however, education wasn't a top priority in my parents' playbook. I attended a comprehensive school in nearby Bushmills, a town famous for Irish whiskey and the world heritage site of the Giant's Causeway. I wasn't pushed academically. In my final year of school, at the age of 16, the allure of the Royal Air Force (RAF) beckoned, and I enlisted before completing my school exams. Excitement took precedence, and finishing school took a back seat. With no GCSEs or A-levels, I left school in 1987 and joined the RAF as an assistant air traffic controller.

First, I received my basic training in RAF Swinderby and then moved to receive my air traffic training in RAF Shawbury. After basic and initial trade training, I was assigned to RAF Kinloss, in Scotland's north coast. I found myself immersed in the dynamic world of the airfield control tower, in the centre of the occasionally busy runway. Kinloss, with its unique charm, ignited a growing fascination within me for aviation.

Directly across from our tower, on a bustling taxiway, sat a civilian flying school. This school, specialising in two-seater Cessna aircraft, welcomed anyone with a thirst for the skies. Their weekend flights became my regular spectacle, each take-off, aerial loop around the aerodrome and meticulous dance of landing practice captivated me. I was utterly enthralled, prompting me to enrol in their programme.

My initial foray into civilian piloting unfolded right there at RAF Kinloss. The instructors, two seasoned Jaguar jet pilots, offered their expertise on their off days from RAF duties. I spent many hours with them in the sky, no doubt run of the mill for them, but top excitement for me. When duty called the instructors overseas, my training shifted to another civilian academy at Dalcross Airport, in Inverness. Dalcross was a good 20 miles from my home, and, rather paradoxically, I hadn't yet learned how to drive at that time. Yes, the irony isn't lost on me. I was mastering the skies before mastering the roads.

Undeterred, my journey to Dalcross for pilot training involved hitchhiking there and back, an adventure in its own right. You might be surprised at the kindness of strangers. I seldom waited more than 20 minutes for a lift, highlighting the generous spirit of the people I encountered, each lift bringing me closer to my dream of becoming a pilot. In April 1990, I sat my final flight exam and flew both navigation and competency flight tests. When I landed, I was congratulated on becoming a pilot. Wow, although I'd successfully passed initial and trade training in the RAF, I considered getting my pilot's licence to be my real first achievement in life, as no one else was driving it.

Amid all this excitement, I was still lacking something: a formal education. I firmly believe education opens multiple doors to positive opportunities. So, when still in the RAF, I devised a plan that would start me on the road to university and a full-time education. Step 1, leave the RAF, much to my parents' disbelief. Step 2, obtain the qualifications to get into university. Step 3, get a job that pays decent enough wages to be able to save sufficient funds for use when at university. I left the RAF, signed up for home correspondence courses and night classes for GCSEs and 'A' levels and applied for a job welding oil rigs for the North Sea.

In mid-1990 I started training to be a welder, building North Sea oil rigs. After months of training, I qualified and began work as a welder at a fabrication yard near Inverness. It was a well-paying job, and I clocked in as much overtime as possible, building a savings pot for my university dream. Welding the joints of an oil rig was a gruelling job. Climbing into confined spaces wearing breathing apparatus to weld joints in scorching temperatures was the norm, as the metal had to be pre-heated to over 100 degrees to ensure it didn't crack. I often emerged, drenched in sweat, to the open-air Highland surroundings where snow on the ground and sub-freezing temperatures was routine. It was a vivid lesson in what I didn't want to do for the rest of my life. A great life lesson if I ever wondered whether my path to a formal education was the correct one.

I studied for the required exams at night and was picked up for my welding shift in the morning at 4.15 am. Exams passed and money saved, I was accepted into two universities, one located in Aberdeen and the other in Edinburgh. It was a challenging time. The fabrication yard started mass redundancies the very month I left, and it's no longer in existence. I welded for two years, and in September 1992 I commenced my law degree at Napier University, Edinburgh.

The four years in Edinburgh pursuing an honours degree in law were nothing short of fantastic. I embraced the city's vibrant life, attending every theatre and concert hall possible. I studied alongside some wonderful fellow students and made some great friends; unfortunately, I don't know where they are today.

I graduated from Napier University in July 1996 with a first-class honours degree in law. I was more than delighted about that, as I had grafted from morning to night, studying to achieve a good result. I'm still proud of the 1990s me who managed to achieve that. That grit and determination not to accept second best has followed me throughout my life. I often make mistakes, and I have had businesses that have failed in my eyes, but they didn't fail because there was a lack of effort or determination on my part. There has never been a truer expression that you don't learn from your successes, only your mistakes and failures.

I graduated in July 1996 and then completed a postgraduate diploma in law from the College of Law, York, from 1996 to 1997. At this stage, I decided that I wanted to pursue a career as a barrister rather than work as a solicitor, so I applied to and was accepted onto a postgraduate diploma in professional legal studies (colloquially known as 'the Bar course') at the Inns of Court School of Law, London. I studied there from 1997 to 1998 as a member of the Honourable Society of Lincoln's Inn. I was eventually called to the

Bar in England and Wales in 1998 and then called to the Bar in Northern Ireland later that year.

I did apply for and was accepted for a pupillage within a chambers in London, next to the High Court on The Strand, but one morning I was standing inside a broken-down train for two hours in 30-degree heat, just 15 metres from London Bridge Train Station platform. There was no room for half the people on that train, no room to stand, no air, no space, everyone crushed in. Because of that incident, and the thought that this could be a regular occurrence if I remained in London, I turned down the offer from the London chambers and applied to be called to the Bar in Northern Ireland. I wanted a slower pace of life and not so many commuters to have to deal with on a daily basis … Belfast bound.

My career as a barrister-at-law spanned a decade, from 1998 to 2008, during which I appeared in courts at all levels – Small Claims Courts, County Court, Crown Court, High Court, Court of Appeal, the House of Lords (now the Supreme Court) and the European Court of Human Rights in Strasbourg.

Being a barrister was intense to the point of keeping me away from my three beautiful children. Leaving for work when they were asleep and returning when they were back in bed became a regular routine. But as a self-employed barrister, the equation was simple: work paid the bills, no work meant no income. The fast-paced nature of the career involved court appearances, research, opinion writing, consultations, negotiations, networking and work-centred socialising. The demanding nature of the job left me with minimal time for my children. I have never been a person who chased money – for me, it was about enjoying what I did – and my priorities became clear. The choice was between becoming a successful barrister or an involved, loving father. Easiest decision I've ever made: the latter. I bid farewell to the Bar and dedicated myself to spending more time with my children.

Being jobless meant I had to find a way to make ends meet. I ventured into starting several companies in my hometown. It wasn't a walk in the park, but, step by step, I was not only building businesses but also investing time in my children. Picking them up from school, strolling along the beach and creating wonderful memories became a cherished routine. To parents reading this, a message: cherish every moment with your small children, as their time with you is limited. Make every interaction count. Find excuses to spend time with them – camping, beach days, treks, picnics or just a stroll in the park. Talk, laugh, make friends and build strong bonds. Your children are your greatest asset. Love them, cherish their company and create a foundation of love and compassion. Your children absorb everything around them and develop based on your treatment of them. Show them that laughter is essential, share in their laughter, invest time in them and cultivate a deep, lasting connection. Remember, children are incredibly perceptive, soaking up everything like little sponges. The way you interact with them shapes their growth. Nurturing them with love and empathy and teaching them the value of joy and laughter are the building blocks of the compassionate, well-rounded adults they will become.

Soon, they'll embark on their own journeys, and you'll long to relive those moments. When my last child went to university, it was lovingly made clear that my role was now 'merely advisory' – a bit of a knock to my dad-ego, but that's exactly what happens. I accepted this role as part of life's travelator and after some soul-searching decided to seek out a new adventure for myself.

My path has always been to resist the urge to conform blindly to societal norms. Embrace a dash of rebellion, carve your unique path and, once you do, pursue it with unwavering dedication and purpose. Strive to ensure each moment is meaningful and not wasted. Approach life as if on a quest to craft the most extraordinary existence possible. Remember, no one else will sculpt your ideal life for you. You're the artist of your canvas, constantly improvising and adapting. Life is a mission to create the best version of you, and you're the one making it up as you go along. Be a bit crazy, but always have some sort of a plan.

Chapter 3
Taking on the Dark Side and Off I Go

This book is a positive and yet realistic chronicle of my first year in Tuscany, but I do have to give you a little background about the true me. We all know that life is a complex series of multiple experiences, and, for some, they have the challenges of physical and mental disabilities. My burden – at least I thought it was a burden – was recognising and battling depression. I had spent most of my life grappling with this invisible adversary, only to confront it head-on in my late thirties. My particular story is one of denial, self-destructive coping mechanisms and the eventual path towards acceptance, treatment and the restoration of meaningful connections.

My struggle with depression began at a young age, though I remained unaware of its presence for many years. As the weight of the darkness intensified, I found myself compensating through various means. One of the most prominent crutches was alcohol, a temporary escape that only deepened the shadows in the long run. I mistakenly believed it to be a remedy for any emotional pain. The numbing effect it provided seemed like a brief respite from the storm within, but it was merely a temporary solution with negative longer-term consequences. I have never been an alcoholic, but when I did drink, I didn't know when to stop. The more I overindulged, the further I distanced myself from the reality of my mental health.

Another way I coped with my inner turmoil was avoiding any form of negativity. This included conflicts, disagreements and even the discomfort of addressing my mental health. I developed a tendency to cut ties with friends and family at the slightest hint of a disagreement, inadvertently isolating myself in a misguided attempt to shield my occasionally fragile emotional state. My propensity to sever relationships without a second thought left a trail of broken connections in its wake. Friends and family, bewildered by my sudden disappearances, were left wondering what had gone wrong. Little did they know that my actions were fuelled by an unconscious, and I stress unconscious, desire to protect myself from any potential emotional harm. My depression developed as an aspect of my personality and manifested itself as a defensive mechanism. This has caused me to train myself to only allow positivity in my life. Positive things, positive people, positive issues. I either simply run away from negative people and situations, or, if needed, face them boldly and make sure they never step into my life again.

It took maturity and a dawning that the constant darkness cannot be real life for me to confront the reality of my problematic mental health. The turning point came when I finally acknowledged that avoidance was no longer a sustainable coping mechanism. I sought professional help and began the journey towards understanding and treating my depression. Acceptance brought clarity and a determination to rectify the situation. I now know that I simply have a chemical imbalance in my brain, and I correct that with tablets. I know the medication is working because if I miss a few days' worth, my mental health crashes – and I mean crashes, worse than I've ever experienced. When on the tablets, I smile and positively bounce out of bed because this is who I truly am. The tablets don't give me happiness and optimism; the tablets rebalance my chemicals and give me back me.

I vividly recall an interaction with a former partner, who reminded me of a moment when I first began my medication for depression. One evening, I said, 'Is this what normal human beings feel like and see?' For the first time, the oppressive dark clouds that had lingered over me had dissipated, leaving clarity in their wake. I experienced a sense of happiness, a refreshing lightness and a newfound freedom.

My journey from a lifetime of depression to acceptance and healing was marked by denial, destructive coping mechanisms and the unintended consequences of running from negativity. It is a testament to the resilience of the human spirit and the transformative power of seeking help. If you are thirsty, you drink; if hungry, you eat; if you have a chemical imbalance, you balance – simple. I am not recovering from depression; I have depression and have a cure for it – my tablets. The tablets might not work for everyone, but, after seeking a cure for many years, these tablets suit me. Now, separately, I have to deal with some of the self-destructive tendencies and actions that occasionally happened during my depressive days. Nothing too scandalous – saying things I didn't mean, losing friends over nothing, cutting ties when they should have remained. I have dealt with this guilt for many years, but I've matured enough now to realise that everyone has their shit to deal with and you can't drive a car while looking in the rear-view mirror.

Here's a thought. Setting aside some of the lost relationships that I feel guilty about, would I wave the magic wand to have lived a life without depression? Strange thing is, I'm not sure I would. I have an inner determination not to be restricted by societal conventions. I have fought my whole life to ensure that every opportunity was available to me and latterly to my children. For me, getting an education after I left school, becoming a pilot, gaining a first-class honours degree in law, succeeding as a barrister, climbing Mont Blanc, surviving the 2015 Nepal earthquake, being an amazing dad, being a successful business owner, emigrating, writing a book – something was and is driving me. Something is giving me the metal to do these things and not settle or make do. Depression is part of my character, and I don't think I'd change that. It has been a driving force in my life, instilling in me an incredible self-determination. Having navigated the depths of despair, I've come to appreciate that joy can be found in everyday living. This journey has empowered me to filter out the trivial distractions, the white noise, the trivial dramas and to move forward without looking back.

The seemingly perpetual grey skies and rain in the UK and Ireland spurred my desire for sunnier climes, igniting an adventurous spirit within me. What grander adventure could there be than to uproot and start again somewhere else? The prospect was daunting, yes, but not insurmountable, especially as an empty-nester. The allure of the sun has always been irresistible to me. There's something about sunny weather that invariably brings a smile to my face, a sentiment I believe many share. It warms my soul.

Life, with its many challenges, remains constant, and I was under no illusion that relocating would somehow magically dispel the issues I faced back in the UK and Ireland. However, the promise of basking in the sun's warmth was a tantalising one. Italy beckoned as a possible sun-drenched haven.

Thus began the flurry of preparations. I needed a detailed plan for my life upon arrival in Italy. My days were filled with activity. It was a daring move, but I had made up my mind and there was nothing to deter me from moving forward with it. Thus, everything was settled and, once ready, I filled my battered old car with whatever I hadn't sold or given away and hit the road.

Throughout my life, I've been an avid traveller, journeying to various corners of the globe. In 2013, I embarked on an ambitious climb up Mont Blanc and Gran Paradiso. Two years later, in 2015, I found myself trekking in Nepal, only to turn back a mere 300 metres from Everest Base Camp because one of my party had fallen ill from lack of oxygen. A day later we were caught in the centre of catastrophic earthquakes. These 7.9 and 8.1 magnitude quakes tragically claimed 8,962 lives and injured an estimated 21,952 people.

My adventures continued in 2016 with a wonderful walking trip through Peru to Machu Picchu. From 2015 to 2023, I conquered numerous peaks, each over 3000 feet high, the thirteen in Ireland, the six in England, and I ascended Ben Nevis no fewer than four times. However, this isn't a book about my life. It's about my first 12 months living in Tuscany. So, you'll be pleased to know that you won't be reading about my three broken noses and missing teeth, my experiences delivering cars throughout the USA as a student, nor about my night spent in a jailcell in central Paris. Having lived my 53 years to the full, I felt well-equipped to take on Tuscany. Yet, as it transpired, Tuscany required no handling at all; it just swept me up.

Having hopefully secured a means of income, teaching English, it was time to immerse myself in the Tuscan lifestyle. Tuscany is renowned for its breathtaking landscapes, rich history and profound artistic heritage. It's also celebrated as the cradle of the Italian Renaissance and even the birthplace of the Italian language. The irony of my situation wasn't lost on me. Here I was, in the heart of a region that gave rise to the Italian language, about to teach English to its inhabitants.

Living in Tuscany has been and is an education in itself. Every day is a lesson in its deep-rooted culture and history, offering me a chance to experience life in a place that has been a significant cultural and linguistic contributor for centuries. The thought of diving in headfirst, armed with my language and experiences to share, was both exhilarating and humbling.

The endeavour of starting a new business in the centre of an Italian town when I had not one word of Italian was daunting, but I took it on with positivism and humour. What could go wrong? Teach English to local Italians. I can't speak Italian; they can't speak English. Oh my. I did know that I had to learn Italian. My brain is good at some things and awful at others. It's just not wired for learning a foreign language. I have met people who pick up languages in weeks – that's not me. In fact, I'm at the opposite end of the spectrum to that person.

As the foundation of the Academy was being laid, I ventured into the realm of TikTok, where I started creating short videos. At the time, this platform seemed like a fitting medium for promoting the Academy and attracting prospective students. I started under the name of Toscana English Academy, but after a few videos I realised that Italians weren't going to watch English-language TikToks, even if they were subtitled in Italian. I then ignored the marketing aspect but kept doing the videos as a diary for my children – as a way for them to watch me set up the Academy and start out in Tuscany. I noticed very quickly that others were interested in what I was doing, asking questions and following my daily story. Ten followers turned into 100, then 1,000, then 10,000. The TikTok story just blossomed from there.

I then changed the name to #OldManAbroad and focused on showing anyone who would watch the beauty of Tuscany – and how an empty-nester could make a go of it. This dual approach, simultaneously managing the Academy and sharing my experiences through videos, proved to be a valuable means of documenting my journey.

The doors of the Academy extended a warm and inclusive invitation to all who sought to enhance their English-speaking skills. This welcoming ethos formed the essence of my very first TikTok post, a heartfelt call to join the Academy and embark on a journey of language proficiency in a joyful and engaging environment.

I initially set up an online presence for the Academy, with fancy QR codes and booking systems, but soon realised that this isn't how business is done in rural Italy. I needed to get out and about and be seen. I put my comfortable shoes on and headed out to meet and greet. I distributed advertising leaflets and introductory letters, in Italian, throughout the local community, all the while only being able to say *Buongiorno*. This grassroots approach aimed to spread the word about the Academy, hoping to ignite motivation among potential students. During my outreach efforts, I encountered a warm and welcoming community that bolstered my enthusiasm for the prospect of teaching English to these Italians. My coverage extended not only to Montaione but also to the surrounding areas, casting a wider net for potential students.

In the following days, I contemplated my experience of relocating to Italy. I've encountered a myriad of insights that I feel compelled to share, particularly for those considering a similar move. Italy, known for its distinct reputation in the UK and Ireland, has been a fascinating place for me, a native of Northern Ireland. Holding both British and

Irish passports, I chose to utilise my Irish passport, affirming my membership within the European Union.

A common misconception is the ease of moving within EU countries while holding an EU passport. While travel might be straightforward, residing in Italy, for instance, involves more complexities, such as obtaining residency, which is essential for tasks like buying a car. Navigating through this process, I visited 13 different offices within the space of ten days, seeking the necessary approvals, a journey not yet completed at the time of writing.

Remarkably, every office I visited was an example of Italian courtesy and efficiency. Despite my lack of Italian language skills and residing in an area where English isn't widely spoken, the assistance I received was exceptional. Staff members went out of their way to communicate, often seeking English-speaking colleagues to aid in the process. They appear to take pride in their administrative abilities.

This level of helpfulness starkly contrasts with what I might have expected back in my homeland, as a non-English-speaking foreigner. It's not my intention to cast a negative light on where I come from, but rather to highlight the commendable Italian system. Despite the bureaucracy, which I found to be surprisingly efficient, the kindness and patience of the people within these systems has been remarkable.

My interactions have not been limited to government offices. Even in the local bank, where communication barriers could have been an obstacle, the staff devoted time to ensure I got what I needed, often using computer translation to bridge the language gap. The warmth and helpfulness of its people, despite the bureaucratic hurdles, makes every moment here truly enriching. Italy, with all its complexities and charm, has indeed captured my heart.

Chapter 4
Nepal and the Lessons Learned

On the 25th of April 2015, I was in the Himalayas in Nepal trekking with my sister. We had just attempted to reach Everest Base Camp, but our attempt failed because one of our party suffered from altitude sickness, and we had to urgently evacuate by helicopter. I could see Everest Base Camp in the distance, a mere 300 metres away after our 10-day trek, but we had no choice but to leave. The only remedy for altitude sickness is to descend, so we took an emergency evac. helicopter down to Kathmandu.

When we arrived in Kathmandu, the person from my party was taken to hospital and, as a result of cutting our trek short, I had a few days free to do what I wanted. I decided to explore Kathmandu and the surrounding areas.

On this particular day, I travelled 80 kilometres west of Kathmandu to do some rafting on a local river. The day started normally. We dressed appropriately and caught a bus to the rafting location. Once there, we were issued with safety gear and were given the usual run-through – instructions on what to do if we fell out of the boat, how to paddle, and so on. Thirty minutes into our rafting experience, we were floating along a quiet section of the river; the only noise was from the motorway above to our left about 200 metres away. I then noticed the river starting to bubble as if we were in a boiling kettle. I pointed at it and said to my guide that this was an earthquake. He initially dismissed it – until both sides of the mountain to the left and right of us started to move and fall towards the valley. Cars on the motorway were getting crushed by the rockslides. Some attempted to reverse but merely crashed into the vehicles behind and then they were crushed themselves.

What was happening was a devastating earthquake with a magnitude of 7.9, followed later by another measuring 8.1 – significant seismic events. Nearly 9,000 people were killed, and over 21,000 were injured. Many of the local structures, which were not built to be earthquake-proof, failed to withstand the tremors. Ironically, we had three Swedish seismologists in the raft with us, who had taken the day off from studying earthquakes in the region. They persuaded us to get off the river, as they were expecting a river tsunami to follow the earthquake.

Since I was 80 km to the west of Kathmandu, where my sister was, I wanted to head back there. However, I was advised not to go to Kathmandu under any circumstances because it was heavily damaged. I headed straight for the motorway and waved down the first car that was able to move and was not affected by the rockslide and asked the driver to take me to Kathmandu. He shook his head vigorously until I produced a bundle of dollars. Off we headed.

The scenes I witnessed on the way to Kathmandu were horrifying. Everyone had evacuated their buildings, fearing aftershocks. They filled the streets, trying to stay safe from further tremors. There was no electricity, no lights except fires, no phone coverage, nothing. We arrived in Kathmandu in the pitch dark except for the lights of the vehicle I was in. The driver knew where to go, and he dropped me off as close to my hotel as the roads would permit. I vaguely knew where I was – only a street or two away from the hotel. I used my phone light and building fires as illumination to take me the extra streets. The place had been devastated, and it was quiet. The streets were packed full of people – no doubt in shock – and there was very little sound coming from them. Eventually I got to the hotel and, thankfully, saw my sister waiting there, in the garden. Everyone was in the garden in fear of the building collapsing during an aftershock.

Structures had collapsed all around us. I vividly remember a shop where, that morning, I had bought bananas for my day trip. Now, it was completely destroyed. Earlier that day, at around 6 am, I had seen a young woman and a child playing in the shop – a memory that now contrasted starkly with the ruins before me.

The tremors were regular, occurring almost every hour. The local wildlife, particularly the crows in the trees, felt the tremors before we did. About 15 seconds before, they squawked in a panic, flying from the trees en masse. And 10 to 15 seconds later the earth rumbled.

Despite the frequent tremors, which we had started to feel were manageable, the real danger hadn't passed. At around one in the morning, it began to rain. We were lying in the garden, trying to find some rest amidst the chaos. In my naïveté, I convinced myself that the worst was over. We had experienced one major earthquake and a few tremors – surely that was it. Wet and uncomfortable in my gear, I decided to go back to my room.

I was staying on the third floor of the hotel. I jumped on top of my bed, still with my clothes on, and quickly fell asleep. At about two in the morning, I was jolted awake by the building violently shaking – an 8.1-magnitude earthquake was tearing through the area. The entire building swayed, moving back and forward dramatically. My wardrobe crashed down onto my bed, the bathroom tiles shattered to the ground, cracks ripped through the walls like a scene from a Steven Spielberg movie. The sounds of glass smashing and people screaming filled the air. I jumped out of bed. The door had already popped open, twisted out of its frame by the force of the earthquake. I rushed out, hurrying down the concrete stairs as cracks seemed to chase me, spreading rapidly along the walls. It was like being in a movie, with the disaster unfolding in real time around me.

I burst out of the hotel doors into the garden. To my left, right and behind me, buildings were collapsing, sending plumes of dust into the air, and the sound of people screaming echoed everywhere. Then, suddenly, silence – a haunting, heavy silence that fell over the area as the dust settled and the screams faded.

After the initial shock, everyone's focus turned to survival and helping others. With buildings all around us severely damaged and continuing to pose a threat because of ongoing tremors, the situation was perilous. The following day, despite the persistent danger and aftershocks, I ventured out in search of water, as we had run out. No water was to be found anywhere. It then dawned on me … if the locals had no water for what they perceived as a rich Western tourist, it meant they had likely run out of water for themselves a lot earlier. Without water, I knew problems were inevitable. It wasn't long before signs of unrest began to emerge. There was some violence, and you could hear looting as people desperately tried to get water and supplies from shops.

With no internet or telephone connection available, we were cut off. In search of a solution, I went into the hotel's library to look for a map. The staff had already deserted it. There were no English books, but I stumbled across an old German travel guidebook about Kathmandu. At the back of this book was a map and the location of the British Embassy. I told my group to wait while I ventured out to find the embassy.

Navigating the streets was a surreal experience – buildings had collapsed everywhere, people were scattered throughout and downed electricity pylons added to the chaos. The scene was a complete and utter mess, exactly as you would imagine in the aftermath of such a disaster.

When I finally reached the British Embassy, there was a queue of about a hundred people waiting outside. I approached a man at the back of the line to ask what was happening, but he didn't speak English, and I realised that this was a queue is of people who did not hold a British passport. I went straight to the front and pressed my British passport against the window. The security officer noticed, gestured urgently and said, 'You, inside.' They opened the large steel security door for me. I quickly asked what time they closed, and he replied, 'We're the British Embassy; we don't close.' … 'I'll be back.'

Relieved, I hurried back to collect my group. 'Grab your stuff – we're going,' I told them. We quickly gathered our belongings and headed back to the embassy. Again, I showed my passport at the front, the doors were unlocked, and we were allowed inside. Once inside, one of our group collapsed with pure relief. We had found safety and refuge. For the next five days, about 200 of us lay on the grass within the embassy compound, waiting for help. Finally, the British Government organised an emergency evacuation flight, and we were flown back to Stansted five days later. This intense experience highlighted the crucial role embassies can play in crises – providing a safe haven and a way out when disaster strikes.

One of the most poignant memories from this ordeal, which will stay with me forever, involves the remarkable support we received during our five-day stay at the British Embassy. We were about 200 people, and, incredibly, we were looked after by just three British Gurkhas, including a colonel and two other ranks. The commitment and resourcefulness of these three individuals were nothing short of heroic.

At one point the colonel shared with us that Whitehall had explicitly instructed him not to open the doors to any additional people outside the embassy. Despite this, many EU citizens, about 150 to 200 of them, gathered outside our gates after being failed by their own embassies. In a moment that defined true leadership and compassion, the colonel, contrary to the orders, decided to open the embassy doors, allowing those 150 to 200 EU citizens into the sanctuary of the British Embassy. It was a bold move, one that he made in the spirit of humanitarian aid – saying, 'Don't tell anyone,' before he quietly let them in.

His actions were not just about offering a safe space; they were about affirming a commitment to human dignity and safety in the midst of a crisis. The relief and gratitude among those who were let in was palpable – they were safe, at last, from the chaos that raged outside. This sanctuary became a place of refuge for many who otherwise had nowhere else to turn.

Outside the embassy walls, the situation remained tense because of the shortage of essential supplies such as water. However, an unexpected bout of torrential rain one night provided a brief respite.

The rain helped to quell the brewing troubles as people hurried to collect the precious water in any containers they had, turning their tent villages into makeshift water collection points. This sudden availability of water dampened the desperation that had driven the looting and unrest. It was a natural reprieve that brought much-needed calm.

Reflecting on these events from my current perspective in Tuscany, I find a deep sense of appreciation for the tranquillity and safety of my surroundings. The 25th of April is a date that not only reminds me of the fragility of life but also reinforces my gratitude for the new chapter here in Italy. I often think about those who were injured in the earthquake and hope that, like me, they have found recovery and a new lease of life since those harrowing days.

I understand this chapter may have carried a solemn tone, but it was the tragedy that unfolded at that time. I could not have defined it any other way. Reflecting on my experiences, I can say that I have come to cherish several valuable lessons that have significantly shaped my optimistic outlook on life. Each of these lessons serves as a reminder of the resilience and capacity for kindness that we, as humans, possess – qualities that are often most visible in times of crises.

Firstly, I learned the importance of community and solidarity. In the face of disaster, the strength of the community is immeasurable. Witnessing people coming together and helping each other with whatever little they had reinforced my belief in the inherent goodness in people. This sense of community doesn't just apply in times of crises; it's a fundamental human need that permeates all aspects of our lives, nurturing our mental and emotional health. It taught me that, no matter where I am, building and sustaining community connections can provide a network of support and shared joy.

Another lesson is the value of resilience and adaptability. Life is unpredictable, and sometimes, despite all our plans and preparations, we are thrown off course. A family friend of ours used to say 'Man plans; God laughs', and it's true. Instead of resisting change, I learned to embrace it, adapting to new circumstances with a positive mindset. This approach has not only helped me navigate difficult times but also opened up opportunities for growth and new experiences. Embracing change leads to a more fulfilling life, where each twist and turn adds to the richness of our personal story.

Furthermore, I discovered the profound impact of acts of kindness. During those harrowing days, the actions of a few, particularly the Gurkhas and the colonel at the British Embassy, highlighted how powerful a simple act of kindness can be. These moments of generosity and courage under pressure reminded me that our actions can be a beacon of hope to others. Living with a mindset focused on what we can give, rather than what we can get, transforms not only our own lives but also the lives of those around us.

The crisis also highlighted the significance of preparedness and awareness. Understanding your environment and being prepared for the worst-case scenario can make a significant difference in outcomes. I've carried this preparedness mindset into all aspects of my life, from personal finance to health and even relationships. It's about being proactive, not reactive, which ultimately leads to greater peace of mind – e.g. ensuring my children always carried an emergency fiver.

Lastly, the experience underscored the importance of cherishing every moment and living life to the fullest. The fragility of life, so starkly revealed during the earthquake, reminded me that each day is a gift not to be taken for granted. This realisation has encouraged me to live more fully, embrace more warmly and express gratitude more freely. It has taught me to find joy in the simple things, seek adventure, learn continuously and ensure that my days are filled with the things that matter most. These lessons have woven themselves into the fabric of my life, guiding me to a more positive, optimistic and fulfilling existence. They remind me that, even in the darkest times, there is light to be found, lessons to be learned and hope to be had. Life is a beautiful journey of constant learning and loving, and each experience, good or bad, is a vital part of that journey.

Chapter 5
Montaione and Surrounding Areas

If you ever come to Montaione, it will reveal itself emerging on the horizon, first the church tower and then a cluster of terracotta rooftops perched on a hill – the quintessential Tuscan village brought to life. It is a town where I immediately thought I belonged.

There is a striking quietness here, a stillness that starkly contrasts with the relentless pace of life I had left behind. Here, time seems to ebb and flow with the rhythm of the seasons, unhurried and unconcerned with the demands of the modern world. The simplicity of this existence resonates deeply within me, stirring a sense of longing and belonging at the same time. But don't confuse simplicity with leaving the modern world behind. Fibre optic Wi-Fi is in abundance, potholes are dealt with quickly and amazon delivery drivers are never away from the town.

The town sits like a gem in the heart of Tuscany, nearly 400 metres above sea level, framed by the rolling hills and expansive skies of the region. The land around the town is rich with the deep greens of vineyards, olive groves and sunflower and lavender fields that sweep gently across the landscape. The hills rise and fall in soft undulations, and every turn reveals a new vista, an endless patchwork of fields and forests, bordered by rows of cypress trees that stand like natural sentinels. It is a landscape that feels timeless.

The town itself offers sweeping views of the surrounding countryside and beyond to the stunning Tuscan Apennine mountains. Its narrow streets and stone buildings blend naturally into the environment. I often just dander around the town to take in the culture and atmosphere that has been like this for centuries. The light in Montaione is something truly special. At dawn, the sun spills over the hills, casting a warm, golden glow over the landscape. By midday, the sun is high, illuminating the vineyards and olive groves in vibrant shades of green, while the evening light softens the hills into a hazy, golden orange.

The land surrounding Montaione is vast and fertile. Vineyards stretch for miles. During August and September, there are rows of grapes ripening in the warm Tuscan sun, while olive groves spread out across the hillsides in neat columns. These fields, alive with the promise of harvest, seem to hum with quiet activity as they slowly transform under the care of the farmers who tend them. In every direction, the hills are dotted with small farmhouses and agriturismos, their stone walls blending naturally with the surroundings, giving the area an air of quiet seclusion.

The roads leading into Montaione are quiet, winding through the countryside with only the occasional car or cyclist passing by. There is no rush, no noise, just the occasional chirp of birds or the rustle of leaves in the breeze. The landscape here encourages a slower pace, a rhythm of life that is in perfect harmony with the environment. It is a place to breathe deeply, to take in the beauty that surrounds you and to savour the stillness.

Montaione and its surrounding areas offer a kind of peace that is rare to find in the modern world. The beauty of the land creates an atmosphere of serenity and tranquillity. This is Tuscany at its finest, a place where you can reconnect with nature and experience a simpler, more peaceful way of life.

The climate in Tuscany plays a crucial role in the success of the harvest. The warmth of the Italian sun, combined with the cooling breezes that sweep through the surrounding hills, creates the ideal conditions for growing both grapes and olives. The sun shines gently over the land, warming the earth and encouraging the plants to thrive. The heat is never overwhelming, thanks to the fresh breezes that cool the air. This balance of sun and gentle wind is what makes the region's climate so perfect for cultivating these crops. But don't forget it does rain occasionally. Tuscany doesn't get this green for lacking water. The night storms can be truly apocalyptic but wonderful.

Tuscany's agricultural traditions run deep. For centuries, the cultivation of grapes and olives has shaped the landscape and the culture of the region. Generations of farmers have passed down their knowledge and techniques, preserving the time-honoured practices that have made Tuscany famous for its wines and olive oil. This tradition is not just about growing crops; it is about fostering a relationship with the land, understanding its needs and working in harmony with it. The region's long history of farming has resulted in some of the finest wines and olive oils in the world, both known for their richness and depth of flavour.

The local culture is as rich and inviting as the landscape itself. There's a rhythm to life here, where traditions and festivals mark the passage of time. One of the first things you'll notice as you settle into the area is the central role food plays in daily life. It's not just about eating. It's about celebrating food, about taking time to appreciate the plate, every bite, every flavour, the way it is presented. It's this careful, intentional approach to food that mirrors the pace of life here – slow, deliberate and deeply rooted in the land.

Tuscany's markets, for example, showcase this celebration of their local produce. You'll find farmers and artisans showcasing their work in the main squares, the air alive with the scent of fresh bread, herbs, cheeses, fruits, flowers and meats. There's a palpable sense of pride in the way people sell their goods, whether it's a wheel of Pecorino Romano cheese, a bunch of freshly picked grapes or a presentation of flowers. At these markets, you don't just buy food; you interact with it and the producers. The market itself becomes a social event, where locals chat, loudly, catch up on the news and share recipes, all while gathering ingredients for their next meal.

Tuscan cuisine is built on the principle of simplicity, but that doesn't mean it lacks depth. One of the dishes that quickly became a favourite of mine was the *Bistecca alla Fiorentina*, the famous Florentine steak. The steak is cooked rare, seasoned with little more than salt, pepper and a touch of olive oil, allowing the natural flavours of the meat to shine through. Every meal in Tuscany is like this – unpretentious, yet full of flavour, and always prepared with a level of care that makes it feel like an event.

The pace of food preparation here is what sets it apart. Cooking isn't something to rush through; it's a process to be enjoyed and appreciated. Preparing a meal is an act of mindfulness, where the chopping of vegetables, the stirring of sauce and the slow simmering of stew becomes a form of meditation. It's a lesson in patience, a reminder that good things take time. This philosophy of slow, deliberate preparation extends beyond the kitchen and is mirrored in the way life is lived in Tuscany. Generally, the people here don't rush. They appear to savour their days, taking the time to enjoy the little things. They are extremely hard workers, but they also know that it is more important to spend time with family during long and, for me, late evening meals.

Beyond the town itself, the surrounding towns and villages offer their own unique glimpses into Tuscan life. A short drive from Montaione takes you to nearby towns such as Peccioli, Volterra or San Gimignano. San Gimignano (good luck pronouncing it) has beautiful medieval towers standing proudly above the landscape. The town feels frozen in time, with its cobblestone streets winding past ancient churches and piazzas that are untouched by modernity. Walking through San Gimignano, you can't help but feel like you're living in a history book. It is probably the most popular town visited by my guests.

Similarly, the town of Certaldo, known for its charming narrow streets and ancient fortress, Certaldo Alto, offers a more intimate look at rural Tuscany. A quiet walk through its old town evokes a sense of peace, with its narrow streets and beautifully preserved architecture creating a perfect harmony between the past and the present. These towns are more than just places to visit; they are living, breathing records of history, where the past continues to shape the way people live today.

But it's the hidden gems that are the real treasures. The small, quiet cafés tucked into corners, offering panoramic views over the vineyards. The artisan shops where local crafts are sold, from leather goods to hand-painted ceramics, each piece made with care and skill. These are the places that give the area its soul, places that allow you to pause and reflect on the beauty that surrounds you. They offer a chance to slow down, just as the land itself does, and experience Tuscany in a way that feels both personal and timeless.

In Montaione and the villages nearby, you're not just a visitor; you're part of something much larger, a way of life that values simplicity, tradition and connection to the land. The culture here invites you to pause, to appreciate the little things and to live at a pace that is in tune with the natural world. It's a place where every meal, every conversation and every view is a discovery, an invitation to experience the fullness of life as, in my opinion, it was meant to be lived.

The Via Francigena (the Italian version of the Camino de Santiago) passes by Montaione. Generally, there is an enthusiasm for walking here, for getting out into the Tuscan hills for a hike. When doing so, you can't help but feel the vastness of nature, offering both a sense of freedom and a sense of peace. The many trails wind through dense forests of oak and pine, their canopies filtering the sunlight onto the forest floor. The air is crisp and clean, carrying the scent of wildflowers and the faintest hint of wild herbs growing along the paths. As you walk, the silence is powerful, broken only by the occasional chirp of a bird or the soft rustling of leaves as a gentle breeze sweeps through the trees. It's the kind of silence that invites introspection, that creates a space for your thoughts to wander.

With each step, the noise of the world recedes, and you're left alone with your thoughts, finding answers to questions you hadn't even known you were asking. The hills, the trees, the sky, they all seem to guide you inward, helping you tap into a part of yourself that might otherwise remain hidden. This solitude is a rare gift. It's not the loneliness of isolation, but the kind of solitude that allows you to hear your own voice more clearly, to reconnect with a deeper self.

In many ways, the hills around Montaione have become a mirror for my own journey of self-discovery. The more time I spend here, the more I feel a deep connection to the land, as though its ancient wisdom is seeping into me, helping me to understand myself in new ways. There's a spiritual quality to Tuscany that can't be easily explained, but it's undeniable once you experience it. Perhaps it's the way the land has been shaped over millennia, or the way it seems to carry the echoes of the past in its very environment. But there's something here that speaks to the soul, something that feels both timeless and transformative.

Italy is a land that has witnessed the rise and fall of civilisations, and their presence is still felt here in the ruins of ancient cities, in the remnants of Roman design and in the quiet stone buildings that are around every corner. This is a place where history isn't confined to the past. It is alive and everywhere. The land's deep connection to its past gives it a sense of permanence, a timeless quality.

Here, I've found more than just a place to live. I've found a backdrop for my own personal transformation. This region – with its beautiful countryside, deep historical roots and unhurried pace – has given me the space to grow. Here, I can reflect and develop parts of myself that I once thought were weak where I came from. Thankfully, those areas are getting stronger as each day passes, revealing the true me. Tuscany has become not just a place to visit but one that has shaped me, much as it has shaped countless generations before me. It is a land that welcomes change, but does so gently, allowing time and nature to do their work. And in this way, it has become a mirror for my own journey, steadily moving forward, one step at a time.

In all honesty, when I pulled into a car park in Montaione in 2023 in my battered car, with everything I owned in the world in my boot, I didn't know what the future held for me – it was frightening but exciting. As I write, it's been just over a year since I made that decision, and I haven't regretted a single moment. The stunning area, magnificent people and amazing climate are everything I dreamt of, and more. But remember, it's not all candyfloss and unicorns. The language has been and still is a formidable challenge, especially for someone with an old brain like mine. The bureaucratic red tape? A test of patience. Earning a living? Still a constant focus. Yet, despite the hurdles, I feel alive in a way I haven't for years. Opening my small English Academy, welcoming visitors and settling into this new life, they all affirm the choice I made to emigrate. If the me today could speak to the me standing on the promenade in Portrush during a storm in July 2023, on my 53rd birthday, questioning what I should do, I'd advise a resounding 'Go for it!'.

Chapter 6
Henrietta, Markets and my Red-Tape Nemesis

As I write these words, I find myself a couple of months deep into what can only be described as a remarkable adventure, one that has officially begun to unfold in the stunning landscapes of Italy. Gradually, I've been immersing myself in the local customs, which have been nothing short of a revelation. It's like being showered with an avalanche of novelties. Now, I could view this deluge as either overwhelming or, as I prefer, an opportunity to go with the flow, drink it all in and personally evolve. This philosophy of embracing the unknown and turning it into a chance for growth has been the cornerstone of my life, one of exploration and discovery. For me, this wasn't so much a challenge but a thrilling adventure.

On arriving here with a large dose of apprehension about driving in Italy, a particularly striking initial observation was the remarkable composure of Italian drivers. Italian drivers have a reputation in the UK and Ireland for being impatient and erratic. Their patience and respect on the road, especially compared to the more hurried pace I was accustomed to, was quite the eye-opener. In rural Tuscany, the deference shown to pedestrians is exemplary. The moment someone hints at crossing the road, vehicles halt. It's a practice I greatly admire and wish was more widespread.

In the absence of a car of my own – I'm not allowed to buy a car because I am not officially a resident – I've unofficially rented 'Henrietta', as I've named her, a battered old Mercedes, and an example of pure resilience and grace under pressure. She is held together mostly by sticky tape and prayers. Despite her age and the tales of wear and tear etched into her frame, she is currently my chariot on the road. Her past may be marked by frequent scuffles, as is the custom here in Tuscany where minor scrapes are met with a shrug rather than confrontation, but she carries it all with an air of dignity.

Henrietta may not be the newest model on the block, but she exudes a charm that's undeniably infectious. Each journey with her, from the quaint cobblestone streets to the twisting and winding roadways, is a chapter in a grand adventure, a reminder of the joys of exploration and the beauty of embracing life's unpredictability. In this picturesque Italian setting, each day is a lesson in appreciation and hope that Henrietta will exit the next corner in one piece and with me still in the car.

My journey so far has unfurled a tapestry of cultural traditions that have quickly endeared themselves to me, chief among them being the weekly market day. Quaint town squares, usually silent and serene, suddenly awaken to the rhythmic clatter of wooden stalls being erected at the break of dawn. These makeshift marketplaces, lovingly organised by the local council, become the pulsating heart of the community once a week, showcasing an array of goods that span the spectrum from vintage attire to artisanal crafts to flowers, fruit, meat and cheese. It's a microcosm of local life, a place where the community's heartbeat is most audible, set against the backdrop of Italy's famously clear, stunning blue skies.

This ritual, I've come to learn, is not unique to my new town but is a cherished tradition across Italy. The central market, a weekly affair, is complemented by smaller, more intimate community markets. Here, local artisans and farmers become the stars of the show, their stalls a kaleidoscope of the region's bounty and craftsmanship. The air is thick with the aroma of fresh produce and the hum of lively chatter creating an ambiance that is both vibrant and soothing. My journey through these markets has been not only a feast for the senses but a fertile ground for social connections.

Among the revelations that I've been delighted to share is the status of the cappuccino as only a morning ritual, a tradition so deeply ingrained that to order one post-noon is to reveal yourself as a foreigner. Then there's gelato, a masterpiece that is not merely ice cream, but something almost divine, unmatched. The gastronomic journey doesn't end with gelato. The Italian cuisine, with its emphasis on fresh ingredients and traditional techniques, has been a revelation – each meal further evidence of Italy's rich culinary heritage, offering flavours that linger long after the meal has ended.

Equally impressive has been my encounter with Italian hospitality. The warmth and open-heartedness of the people have made every interaction, whether in the bustling markets or the quiet of a local café, a moment of genuine connection. This extends into the realm of public services, where I've encountered a level of professionalism in bureaucracy that has made navigating the intricacies of residency and other formalities an efficient but never-ending experience.

Adapting to the local customs, such as the late dinner times and the midday pause when towns seem to take a collective breath and retreat into their homes, has been an exercise in cultural immersion. These customs, reflective of a lifestyle that prioritises family and well-being over the incessant rush of productivity, have been both a challenge and a charm to which I've had to adapt. The leisurely pace of life – where family and community take precedence and every meal is an opportunity for togetherness – has been a wonderful change to my previous hurried existence. Embracing this slower, more deliberate pace of life is an ongoing journey, one that I undertake with a sense of anticipation and openness.

In sum, my Italian odyssey has been a mosaic of new experiences, culinary delights and social rituals, each piece a cherished memory in the making. As I continue to immerse myself into this vibrant culture, I look forward to the discoveries that await, each day a step deeper into the heart of Italy. For anyone contemplating a move to this enchanting part of the world, be prepared for a delightful, albeit significant, adjustment period. The local customs and lifestyle practices, while charming, might necessitate a period of adaptation.

Adjusting to life here, however, extends beyond customs and habits. The process of establishing residency, for example, is a journey through a labyrinth of bureaucratic requirements that can be as daunting as it is critical. I have a love/hate relationship with Italian red tape – I hate it, and they love giving it to me.

Nestled in my apartment, I have a stack of documents, each a vital key to unlocking my new life here. The following are just a few examples: my passport and international driver's licence – the latter an indispensable necessity for navigating Italy's picturesque but sometimes challenging roads. Equally crucial was securing a local bank account to facilitate all manner of financial transactions, from the mundane to the monumental. Then came the *Codice Fiscale* – akin to a national insurance number – an essential piece of identification without which everyday life, from securing a mobile phone plan to joining a local library, would be inaccessible.

The list extended to include the *numero di Partita IVA* – Italy's version of a VAT number – vital for anyone looking to engage in business or professional activities, and a PEC (*posta elettronica certificata*) address. This secured email account is a prerequisite for the legal exchange of documents and invoices, embedding itself as a cornerstone of both professional and bureaucratic communication.

A proof of accommodation – whether through a lease agreement or property ownership – was another hurdle, required to demonstrate that I had a stable base and wasn't living out of a box. And then there was the matter of health insurance. Regardless of your status as a European Union citizen, private health insurance is a non-negotiable requirement for a residency application, a policy that underscores that you won't be a burden on their health service. The financial sustainability clause was yet another requirement in the country's meticulous residency application process. It wasn't enough to simply wish to reside in this beautiful country; you had to demonstrate the means to live independently, without relying on state resources.

Amidst this whirlwind of paperwork and preparation, I encountered terms and requirements that were entirely foreign to me, such as the digital signature protocol, a concept I'm gradually unravelling. The road to residency is indeed paved with challenges, but for those willing to navigate its course, the rewards are as profound as the country's storied history and breathtaking landscapes.

My journey into the heart of Tuscany has been an eye-opening experience, revealing the exceptional nature of the local people and their meticulous approach to daily life. The handling of paperwork, a task that can often be mundane and frustrating, was executed with such precision and care here that it left me in awe. The volume of documents required for various applications was immense, enough to overwhelm anyone, yet the officials managed it all with a level of patience and efficiency that was nothing short of remarkable.

This exemplary approach wasn't limited to government offices alone. When it came time to set up Wi-Fi for the Academy, I encountered the same rigorous attention to detail. The service providers required a copy of some of the same documents, and they handled them with the same level of care and commitment to service. The promise of having Wi-Fi installed within a week to ten days was yet another example of the incredible efficiency that seems to permeate all aspects of life here, so far. Wi-Fi was installed within five days. What has impressed me most is this consistent dedication to excellence – a reflection of the locals' commitment to quality in everything they do.

The organisational skills of the Tuscan people are truly unparalleled. Their approach to queuing, for instance, is a marvel of efficiency and fairness. Whether in a public office or a bustling supermarket deli, the system of taking a number and waiting for your turn is adhered to with a level of discipline that surpasses even the famed British queues. This structured approach to service and fairness extends throughout the community, ensuring a smooth and orderly process in all public dealings.

Immersing myself in Italian culture and taking steps to learn the language have been at times the most exhilarating and frustrating parts of my adventure. The warmth and openness of the local people has allowed me to explore new places, meet fascinating individuals and forge meaningful friendships. I started to become recognised, which led to an unexpected honour – an invitation to a local football match featuring the local team, Aurora Montaione. On arrival at the stadium on a warm Sunday afternoon, I was presented with a team shirt and scarf. Donning the team shirt, I mingled among the passionate fans, jokingly hoping not to be mistaken for one of the players – although my stomach poking out of the bottom of the shirt would dispel any confusion.

This opening match of the football season was an event that captured the essence of local sportsmanship and community spirit. As I joined the home supporters, the intense Tuscan sun added an extra layer of fervour to the already electric atmosphere, with temperatures soaring to a sweltering 32° – and that was just in the stands. But it wasn't just the weather heating things up – the players on the field matched the sun's intensity with their passionate play, resulting in a whirlwind of yellow cards throughout the match. The referee could have easily handed out a few red cards given some of the heated exchanges and aggressive tackling.

The match itself was a nail-biter, with both teams demonstrating skill, determination and a competitive edge that kept everyone on the edge of their seats. The final score, a 1-1 draw, was a fair reflection of the evenly matched tenacity displayed by both sides. After the game, I had the pleasure of speaking with Leandro, one of the coaches for the Montaione team. He shared insights into the team's philosophy, emphasising their focus on nurturing young talent and building a foundation for future generations of footballers in the region. It was heartening to learn about their commitment to development over immediate success, a long-term vision aimed at strengthening the team's core and enhancing their capabilities.

Through these experiences – from navigating the bureaucratic processes to participating in local traditions and sporting events – I've gained a profound appreciation for the Tuscan people. The exceptional organisation, dedication to quality and vibrant community spirit have made my integration into this beautiful region an incredibly rewarding journey. Each day brings new insights and connections, deepening my bond with this enchanting part of Italy.

Another aspect of Tuscan life I've come to cherish is the early-morning culture. Unlike the rushed starts I was accustomed to back in the UK and Ireland, Tuscan mornings are about rising at dawn and embracing the day with a leisurely breakfast hour that sets a serene tone for what lies ahead. This tradition of taking time to enjoy the morning, to relish in the calm and beauty of the early hours, resonates deeply with me as a morning person. The contrast to my previous life – where mornings were a blur of hurried activity and cold grey skies – couldn't be starker.

Embracing this slower start has allowed me to appreciate mornings in Montaione in a way I never could before. The peaceful streets at dawn, the soft light filtering through the Tuscan hills and the time taken to enjoy a quiet morning coffee without the pressure of rushing out the door into the rain have become moments I truly treasure. It's a lifestyle that prioritises well-being and mindfulness. This embrace of early mornings, combined with the vibrant local culture and the thrilling, competitive world of amateur Tuscan football, has made my time here incredibly fulfilling – offering a blend of excitement and tranquillity that I've come to love deeply.

Above: With my parents and siblings, 1980.

Top right: Summit of Gran Paradiso, Italy, 4,061m, 2013.

Right: Summit of Mont Blanc (or if Italian, Monte Bianco), 4,810m, 2013.

Below: Where I now call 'home'.

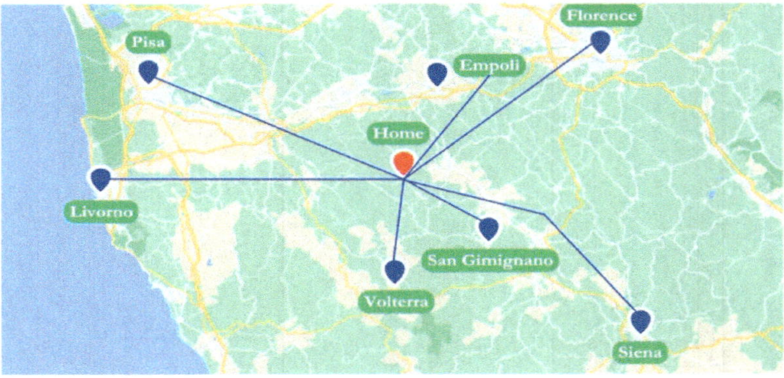

Left: The beautiful town of Portrush on the north coast of Northern Ireland, where I grew up and spent an amazing childhood. All I needed was a wetsuit, a football and a bicycle.

Right: A wine window in Florence used to sell wine directly to the Florentines. Helpful when pandemics forced the closure of direct and open wine sales. Approx. 150 still exist today.

Below: The wonderful town of Montaione where I have settled. The Tuscan Apennines in the rear.

Above: With my sister and Everest in the background, 2015.

Below: BBC coverage of my return to Northern Ireland after nearly two weeks in the Himalayas following the 2015 earthquakes.

Nepal quake survivor Barry Torrens returns home

30 April 2015 | Northern Ireland

Barry Torrens at Belfast City Airport on Thursday night

Below: The remains of the shop where I bought bananas earlier in the day, post first earthquake, 2015.

Below: One day from Everest Basecamp, 2015, 5,000 metres asl.

Above: The Causeway Shantymen, aka The Salty Seadogs, 2023.

Right: My son and I hiking in the Lake District en route to Italy.

Below: My entire worldly possessions after decluttering, day 1 of the move.

Below: The Toscana English Academy before renovations.

Chapter 7
Embracing Italian Culture

It's a bit of a cliché, but us lot from the UK and Ireland are notoriously rubbish at picking up other European languages. I wouldn't want to tar everyone with the same brush, but speaking for my extended family and friends, there's more than a grain of truth in it. In my defence, I'm now giving it a solid but ineffectual go at getting to grips with Italian.

We're also known for a rather peculiar habit: if someone who doesn't speak English doesn't understand what we say, we tend to just up the volume, as if that'll work. I thought it was merely a habit from the UK/Ireland. Nope, I've found myself being at the other end of that here in Italy. I've got this one Italian phrase that's become a bit of a mantra for me: *'Mi dispiace, non capisco l'italiano. Parla inglese?'* It translates to 'I'm sorry, I don't understand Italian. Do you speak English?'. Given that I'm still finding my feet with the language, it's a phrase I use two or three times a day, easily.

When I trot out this line to all the unfortunate souls who have tried to correspond with me, instead of twigging that I'm not fluent in Italian and perhaps easing up, they just repeat themselves – only much, much louder – as if I'd just said, 'I'm terribly sorry, my hearing's not what it used to be. In fact, I'm profoundly deaf, so could you please step well inside my personal space and shout what you've just tried to verbally communicate?' But all things considered, it's all part of the adventure. It's these little quirks that make my stay here all the more memorable. They add a certain '*mamma mia*', making me fall head over heels for Italy and its people. And yes, they do say '*mamma mia*' when they are surprised.

The evening skies here are a spectacle to behold. Each sunset is a masterpiece viewed from my terrace, painting the horizon with colours that'd make a rainbow blush. It's a sight that never grows old, a daily reminder of life's beauty. In the UK and Ireland, where the skies are, more often than not, shades of grey and the rain often constant, such vibrant displays are rare treasures. But here, the skies dazzle with clarity, and the sun bows out each evening with a performance that stirs the soul. I'll never tire of it. This leap from the familiar drizzle to sun-soaked evenings wasn't a decision I made lightly. Uprooting from Northern Ireland to Italy was no small feat, but, as I sit here basking in the warm glow of another sunset, I'm convinced, for now, it was the right one.

The view from my hilltop apartment is beautiful and panoramic. A glance in one direction reveals a vista towards the coastal towns of Livorno and Pisa. When I turn my head to the right, my gaze is towards Florence, tonight backlit by the drama of an approaching storm. The spectacle of lightning brewing in the heart of towering cumulonimbus clouds – these colossal formations heavy with rain – is a stunning display of nature's power and elegance. I love watching the storms. They arrive, perform their show and disappear quickly.

I'm well aware that serene moments can be just a pause within everyday life. My battles with the shadows in my mind have taught me to remain watchful, ready for when the tides turn. But for now, I'm content to lose myself in the spectacle of the sky, finding peace in the beauty of sunsets and storms alike.

It's the simple joys, the ones we've somehow let slip through our fingers back in the UK and Ireland, that breathe life into my days here. We've grown accustomed to the hustle – our eyes glazed over, our spirits dulled to the beauty of everyday interactions. I, too, was guilty of this oversight until my arrival here, where I was gently reminded of a tradition as heartwarming as it is fundamental: the simple act of saying hello to a passing stranger.

Gone are the days, it seems, where a passing glance between strangers would spark a warm exchange of smiles, a chirpy 'Morning'. Now, our paths cross in silence, our gazes fixed ahead, as if the other doesn't exist. But not here in Tuscany. Here, every encounter is an opportunity for connection. A shared glance brings forth a '*Buongiorno*' as bright as the morning sun. This fabric of social warmth is a poignant reminder of what some have lost in our relentless march towards modernity and insularity.

This revival of simple human connection, this rekindling of community spirit, is a beacon of what life was – and still should be – everywhere. In the shadow of ancient Tuscan hills, amongst the olive groves and vineyards, I've found a society that cherishes the very essence of being human: acknowledging, appreciating and celebrating each other's presence.

In my quest to speak Italian, Google Translate has become a trusty, if imperfect, ally. It's a tool that bridges the gap between my fledgling or non-existent Italian and the locals' limited English, enabling exchanges that would otherwise be fraught with confusion and misunderstanding. The app's real-time translation feature has proven invaluable, transforming my smartphone into a makeshift interpreter that facilitates everything from casual banter to crucial conversations.

Yet, as reliant as I've become on this digital crutch, I'm acutely aware of its limitations. The convenience of instant translation comes at a cost – subtly undermining my commitment to learning Italian by providing an all-too-easy escape from the rigours of learning the language. This reliance, I fear, could widen the gap between mere survival communication and true linguistic fluency, turning what should be a steep but rewarding learning curve into an insurmountable cliff. At the time of writing, and no doubt at the time of your reading, I'm still floundering with the language like a toddler learning algebra – I am so useless at languages.

I do a lot of walking as part of everyday Tuscan living. Walking not only serves the practical purpose of counteracting the delicious Italian food that has become a hallmark of my stay, but also provides a much-needed physical outlet – a way to tire my body in preparation for a restful sleep. This simple act of walking – moving at a human pace – offers a meditative counterpoint to the frenetic energy of learning and adapting to a new environment. It's a chance to reflect on the day's experiences, to absorb the sights, sounds and rhythms of Italian life – and, of course, you also get to have a good nosey at things you miss when speeding past in a vehicle.

After a day covering a few kilometres, I find myself grateful not just for the physical tiredness that promises rest but also for the deeper sense of peace that comes from knowing I'm exactly where I need to be. In this land of ancient cities and rolling hills, of art and history and life lived out loud, I'm slowly but surely finding my footing, very slowly learning to navigate the complexities of a new language and culture and discovering the joys and challenges of forging a new life in a place that, day by day, feels more like home. I'm only hoping that it isn't a false dawn.

Waking up to the gentle kiss of the morning sun is a luxury I've come to cherish deeply here. My bedroom, perfectly positioned to greet the dawn, becomes a sanctuary of light each morning. The sun's rays, filtering through the open window, wake me up with a warmth that's both comforting and invigorating. This natural awakening, devoid of the jarring intrusion of an alarm, is a tonic for body and soul.

As the day unfolds and I immerse myself in work and daily chores, I ensure to carve out moments for personal exploration, especially during the customary Tuscan midday break from 1 pm to 4 pm. This pause offers a splendid opportunity to wander and discover the endless novelties this place has to offer. On one such escapade, I stumbled upon a delightful spectacle in a local piazza. The community had transformed the square into an alfresco cinema, ingeniously using a vast plastic sheet strung up on scaffolding as a makeshift screen. This simple yet imaginative setup invited everyone to gather under the stars and share in the joy of cinema, creating a communal experience that was both heartwarming and enchanting.

Such experiences underscore the ingenuity and communal spirit that pervades this place. It's in these moments, surrounded by the laughter and camaraderie of neighbours and friends, that I'm reminded of the profound beauty of simplicity. The ability of this community to create magic from the mundane, to weave joy into the fabric of everyday life, gives you a peek into the endless wonders that await discovery here. Each day is an invitation to take part in a multitude of experiences that make Montaione not just a location, but a home. With every sunrise, every meal, every chance encounter, I find myself more entwined with the essence of this land, forever in awe of the simple pleasure of my days.

The allure of Tuscany extends far beyond its sun-kissed vineyards and rustic charm; it's in the very air you breathe, in the sounds that punctuate the stillness, creating a symphony that resonates with the soul. The profound silence that blankets the landscape is the first of these auditory treasures, a rare commodity in our noisy world. It's a silence that envelops you, a tangible presence that invites introspection and tranquillity. In these moments of pure silence, time seems to stand still, allowing you to savour the essence of peace. This silence isn't merely the absence of noise. It's a moment of pure thought, a sanctuary where the mind can wander unfettered, free from the noise of daily life.

Contrasting with this serene backdrop is the joyful clamour of church bells, a sound that embodies the spirit of the community. The bells, with their rich, resonant tones, mark the passage of time in a melody that's been constant through generations. Each peal – whether calling locals to chapel or celebrating a local festival – is a thread of continuity and tradition in daily life. I love the bells ringing out throughout the countryside, but they are super loud if you are caught inadvertently below the tower. The locals are used to them, but I still jump – much to their amusement.

Tuscany's magic doesn't stop at its soundscape. As you meander through its streets, alleys and piazzas, the region reveals its artistic soul through spontaneous displays of creativity. On a leisurely stroll, you might encounter whimsical art installations that transform the mundane into the extraordinary. Imagine coming across a group of life-sized ballerina figurines, poised as if caught mid-dance, their silent grace revealing the region's enduring love affair with beauty. These installations are not just decorations but conversations between artist and observer – invitations to pause, reflect and appreciate the intertwining of art and life.

Every corner of Tuscany offers a new story, a new reason to fall deeper in love. From the meditative hush that blankets the countryside to the exuberant chimes that echo through its towns, from the rustic cobblestones to the spontaneous bursts of art, Tuscany is simply a masterpiece. As you immerse yourself in this world, every sense is awakened, every moment a brushstroke in the painting of your journey, compelling you to explore further, to discover the boundless wonders that lie waiting in the heart of this captivating land. I've stopped many times to think, 'Wow, they've placed that amazing artwork there purely for the pedestrian's personal enjoyment' – and it works.

Living in a place that holds art in such high esteem, where the balance between functionality and aesthetic beauty is so gracefully maintained, it's hard to imagine ever growing weary of it. Italy, with its rich culture, truly understands the intrinsic value of art and its vital role in shaping a humane society. Art is more than mere decoration; it's the words of a community, a bridge to our deepest selves and a reflection of our collective humanity. In this regard, Italy stands out, ensuring that even the most practical aspects of living are touched by beauty and creativity.

This deep appreciation for art and beauty seems to permeate the Italian character, manifesting in their humility, kindness and compassion. I recently bought a mattress-topper online. When buying online, I usually buy from shops as close as possible to where I'm living. The topper arrived in a regular box, but at the bottom of the box when I took the topper out, there was a bottle of Italian perfume – a gift for buying their goods. It was a touch of elegance, a hint of luxury and a profound statement about the nature of business and customer care in this country. It's not every day that you find a mattress company that sends a bottle of perfume along with your purchase.

This act of generosity, this unexpected gift, was further evidence of the Italian way of life, where even a simple transaction is an opportunity to spread joy and beauty. In Italy, it seems, the pursuit of beauty and the desire to bring joy to others are never far from the mind, making every day an opportunity to encounter the unexpected and the wonderful.

Chapter 8
Wine Windows and an Introduction to TikTok

In Italy, I find that there's something to learn everywhere you look. Take, for example, the way shop assistants juggle multiple customers simultaneously – a bit of a shock to the system coming from the UK and Ireland. I recently waited patiently in a lengthy queue for my Italian mobile phone, and when I was called forward, I eagerly presented all of my documents, hoping that I had everything they needed. The shop assistant looked at the documents, looked passed my right shoulder and said in Italian, 'Next, how can I help you?' I think I let out an audible squeak of disbelief and laughter. He continued dealing with my documents while helping the next customer. This practice, while initially confusing to an outsider, shows wisdom here in embracing the beauty of multitasking and the fluidity of engagement.

In the face of adversity, the people of Tuscany knew that innovation was the key to keeping the gears of life rolling. Take the historical account of the Black Death and the innovative response of the Tuscan vineyard owners with their wine windows – a lesson in resilience and innovation. Faced with a catastrophic pandemic, people found ways to adapt, survive and even thrive. The creation of wine windows – a small hole with a mini door cut into the wall of the vineyard owner's house to sell their product without contact – wasn't just about selling wine; it's an example to human creativity and the drive to find solutions in the face of dire circumstances. The intrinsic wisdom here is a reminder that, even in the darkest times, humanity's ingenuity and determination can light the way forward.

The ability to adapt, to embrace new ways of thinking and interacting, is crucial. It's not about discarding our own methods but about enriching our lives with a diversity of experiences. Like the Italian shop assistants, we can learn to engage with multiple people, sharing our attention in a way that enriches our interactions rather than dilutes them. It's a balance, a dance of presence that, when mastered, adds depth to our connections.

In essence, experiences and historical reflections offer a simple yet profound wisdom. Life is ever-changing, filled with both challenges and joys. Embracing adaptability, engaging with the diverse world and finding creative solutions in the face of adversity help navigate this landscape.

The wine windows still exist in Tuscany, although their numbers have drastically decreased. Today, there are about 150 original wine windows in and around Florence. In my opinion, they are wonderful little things, and coming up with them was a brilliant idea given the circumstances of that time. Even in modern times, these windows have proven their utility, when they were reused during COVID. I don't want to say it was of a similar nature to the old tragedy, but at least the application was identical. During the most recent pandemic, these windows were used to sell wines, coffee, teas and snacks.

As I explore Italy, I keep uncovering new lessons hidden in everyday moments. One of the first things that struck me was how crucial body language is here. In English-speaking countries, we often overlook gestures, but in Italy, they are central to communication. Even without understanding Italian, I've started to 'hear' people through their gestures, learning that there's so much more to conversation than just the words used.

This journey of discovery didn't just stop with learning about communication. It extended to the land itself – the gardens, vineyards and olive groves – where the dedication of gardeners and farmers is evident in every leaf and vine. Here, it's not just about having a green thumb; it's about the love and care poured into the earth. Watching them work, I realise that growing something beautiful requires not just knowledge and skill but also a deep passion.

Deciding to move to Italy was a big step, filled with sacrifices, especially being away from my children. However, modern conveniences have softened the sting of distance. I speak with my children daily using various messaging methods and video calls – something that was impossible when I left home in the late 1980s. In 1987, I had to queue up outside a red telephone box on a Sunday evening to call home, hoping that the person in front wasn't going to be too long. When you entered the phone box, the receiver was warm – and the smell wasn't too good. Also, now, a quick and, if booked wisely, cheap flight can bring me back to my loved ones, making the physical distance seem less daunting and reminding me that pursuing dreams doesn't mean losing connection with those important to me.

The language barrier is my biggest hurdle. After years of studying for my profession, the thought of starting again and learning a whole new skill, i.e. Italian, felt overwhelming. Yet, to my own surprise, I've found joy in the process. I'm slowly – very slowly – picking up the language, mainly driven by necessity in rural Italy. This experience has shown me that even the most intimidating challenges can become semi-enjoyable learning opportunities.

Living in Montaione, surrounded by Italy's stunning natural beauty and rich history, has confirmed I made the right choice. The lifestyle here, from the Vespas buzzing by to the incredible food and welcoming people, has added a richness to my life I hadn't known before. My move to Italy has been more than a change of location; it's been a deep dive into what it means to live fully. It's shown me the importance of listening and connecting beyond words, the value of dedication in nurturing life and the beauty of following your passions despite challenges. Italy has taught me about the strength of connections, the courage to face new challenges and finding joy in new experiences.

Living here has reshaped my perspectives, especially on things I previously dismissed – simple things like looking at nature or the art of making coffee. Back in the UK and Ireland, I couldn't understand the fuss over coffee rituals, happily settling for instant coffee. But Italy changed me. The simple yet profound pleasure of a good espresso has turned me into a coffee enthusiast, nay snob, eager to embrace all the tools and machines necessary for that perfect cup.

My appreciation hasn't stopped at coffee. I find myself increasingly drawn to everything Italian, including the language. Despite its loudness, Italian to me sounds like poetry; however, the musical lilt I hear now might lose its charm as I learn more and become fluent. The Italians think nothing of standing on their balcony while on their phone and speaking to someone hundreds of miles away as if they were merely connected by string. They even put the other person on the speakerphone, loud setting, so we can hear both ends of the conversation – zero secrets here. This might sound like a cop-out, but I do fear losing the romantic nature of the language if I can understand that they are complaining about their most recent haircut or the price of oranges in the Co-op. Yet, learning the language is essential for my life here, a challenge I'm hoping to one day enjoy.

My move to Tuscany was also driven by a desire for simplicity. I used to live in a large house filled with possessions that often – maybe always – felt burdensome. I used to look pessimistically into a garage groaning with miscellaneous clutter that I didn't need. Now, in a much smaller apartment, life is straightforward and uncluttered, which suits me perfectly. This downsizing has been liberating, allowing me to focus on what truly matters. As an empty-nester, I've embraced this simpler lifestyle, finding contentment in having just what I need, nothing more. Prior to moving here, and when I had just moved out of my accommodation, I had a shipping container packed full of items. Every time I thought about it, I felt the world pressing down on my shoulders. One day, I opened the doors of the container, invited some charity shops to lift what they wanted, put a few bits aside to sell and gave the personal items to my children as an early inheritance – zero stuff left for the move apart from underpants and socks.

Living here has prompted me to explore parts of me I never knew existed. For instance, I am genuinely quite a private person. I would never have imagined I would be sharing my local and daily experiences with an audience by making videos on TikTok – or now writing a book. What was primarily initiated for promotional purposes for my small English Academy has turned into me telling the world about this wonderful place, where each little experience is nothing short of an adventure. The more I am taken by surprise, the more I want the world to know how amazing this country is and how wonderful I'm being treated here.

Initially, the videos were just for my children so they would have an update on my life – and only for a very short time as I settled in. But the way my channel exploded took me by surprise. Over the next few months, it grew, providing me with a digital family to keep updated and share my Tuscan adventures with. When you find people who are interested in your experiences and with whom you can connect online – strangers that make you feel like family – well, you have no choice but to oblige and treat them accordingly.

My online base is gradually growing, and I am now using social media to the best of my ability to showcase Italy and its people in their true beauty. Perhaps that is what truly prompts me to appreciate the bounty of Tuscany and realise how fortunate I am to have come here. My journey shows that it's not impossible. I believe anyone can do it with the right research and planning. It suited me at my stage in life, i.e. empty-nester, but it won't suit everyone. As well as wanting to live in the sun, I was also driven by a concern that, if I didn't have a go now, then I might be filled with regret in later years.

Not everyone feels the pull to leave their hometown, but for someone like me, who grew weary of endless grey skies and relentless rain, relocating was a dream come true. It's the inner weather, the climate of the soul, that truly determines my happiness. I've yearned for nothing more than sunny days and clear blue skies for as long as I can remember. If sharing my story through simple one-minute videos or this book inspires even one person to chase their dreams and face life's challenges boldly, then I've achieved what I set out to do. The journey to a new country might seem daunting, but it's entirely feasible. There are steps and formalities, of course, but nothing too overwhelming.

And now, here I am, in a picturesque town in Tuscany, surrounded by endless greenery, under vast blue skies, amidst stunning architecture, enjoying the finest food and meeting the kindest people. I'm well aware that life comes with its share of highs and lows, and I have had many of both. It's not always going to be perfect, and that's fine. That variability is what makes life enjoyable. I'm braced for the occasional stormy day, both metaphorical and with the weather. The occasional heavy rain here is what keeps this place so vibrant and alive, coupled with the sunshine. Having spent decades in the UK and Ireland, I'm no stranger to rain and storms. I've even invested in sturdy weather gear here, ready to face any rainstorm head-on. If enduring a few rainy months means I get to enjoy the rest of the year in this sunny paradise, I say let the rain come.

The range of exquisite wines and sumptuous dishes here is endless, promising a new taste adventure around every corner. However, a word of caution from my own experience: having once tipped the scales at 105 kilograms, I'm mindful of the need for moderation amidst such temptation. The days of youthful exuberance and effortless fitness are behind me, replaced by a slower metabolism that demands caution with my diet. Yet, here's the surprising part, despite living in a place renowned for pizza, pasta, red wine, tiramisu and gelato – unavoidable, I know – I've somehow managed to shed over 15 kilograms. Maybe it's the magic of the Tuscan air, the purity of the water or living outdoors in the sun, but, somehow, indulgence here seems to come with a side of weight loss, a delightful paradox that's just another part of this place's charm.

Regrets are the silent burdens that shadow us into our later years, stirring wonder about the paths not taken, actions taken, words spoken or not spoken, and the dreams not pursued. This reflection springs from a profound insight gained from a report I encountered long ago, which surveyed 100 individuals over 95 years old, asking them what their biggest regret in life was. The overwhelming response was not taking enough risks. This haunting theme of missed opportunities and uncharted ventures has since become a beacon guiding my own journey.

Starting this new chapter in Italy at 53, without a safety net of wealth or a pension, represents my stand against a life of regrets. The challenge of integrating into a community whose language I don't grasp, coupled with the daunting possibility of this entire endeavour not succeeding, would send many retreating. Yet, the alternative, a life of wondering 'what if', clouded with the thought of a life without adventure, motivates me to press forward, embracing the uncertainty with open arms.

My personal motto has always been 'Play by your own rules' – sometimes it works, sometimes it will get you in a lot of trouble, but I'm enjoying where it has landed me now.

My apartment is nestled in the vibrant heart of the Chianti region, a front-row seat to the seasons of wine country. Chianti stretches from Florence through to Pisa and down to Siena, and I find myself at its very core. As harvest season unfolds, the early morning buzz of workers converging on the vineyards becomes a daily spectacle. From dawn 'til dusk, teams of dedicated men and women gather grapes, filling the air with the promise of future vintages. The procession of trucks, heavy with grapes destined for winemaking, is a common sight, a vivid reminder of the region's pulse.

The local wine, particularly Barolo, demands respect, its potent effects an example to the region's craftsmanship. While I savour the occasional glass, my responsibilities necessitate clarity and focus, especially given the bureaucratic necessities that punctuate my life here. The impact of wine at this stage of my life is not to be underestimated. A single bottle can cloud the week ahead – 'a big girl's blouse' as I would be called in my hometown.

Getting my residency was a big moment for me. Even with a European (Irish) passport, it wasn't easy. There are a lot of steps and challenges to overcome to really make a life here in Italy (see Chapter 20: Getting Here Admin). But when I finally got my residency, it felt as if Italy was officially welcoming me. I had to deal with a lot of paperwork and visits to and from the authorities, which I've talked about before. Now, if I stay here for five years, I could apply for Italian citizenship and an Italian passport. This whole experience has been about more than just getting the right to live here; it's been about becoming part of this place that now feels like home. Now let's master the language.

Chapter 9
Starting to Make Headway

In the middle of adapting to a foreign culture and people, finding a friend can be like discovering a treasure. I was fortunate enough to find such a person. If truth be told, he sought me out. I heard a knock on the door as I was painting the Academy, and there he was. He introduced himself as Francesco, or Franco, and said that if I needed anything, anything at all, he was the first stop. If he can't organise to have an Italian issue sorted, it can't be sorted. He has been wonderful from the moment he introduced himself, and I hope to remain close friends with him for as long as I am in Italy and beyond. To be fair, every individual I've met has been nothing short of remarkable.

In my narratives, I may have unintentionally painted an overly idyllic picture of relocating abroad, possibly leading some to believe it's an endeavour devoid of hardships. The reality, however, is that challenges are an integral part of this journey, challenges that I continue to confront head-on. But it's the attitude I choose to take towards these hurdles that truly makes the difference. I've adopted a 'bring it on' mindset, facing each obstacle without hesitation or retreat. This approach has not only allowed me to navigate the complexities of living in a new country but also enriched my experience immeasurably. While the path of moving to a foreign culture is not always puppy dogs and rainbows, the thorns encountered along the way are what make the journey truly memorable and rewarding.

Setting on the path to secure residency here was complex and, frankly, quite draining. Despite the relatively high efficiency for which the Italian bureaucratic system is known, the amount of it is something to behold. I steeled myself with determination, fully aware of the necessity of the ordeal. It felt like a personal challenge between Italy and myself, and I mentally declared 'Oh no, Italy, I refuse to be defeated in this encounter'. The difficulty of the process did not deter me. On the contrary, it only strengthened my resolve not to retreat. I was firmly set on being the architect of my own fate. I was not going to be put off by the enormity of the red tape mountain that Italy is famous for, but rather I was determined to scale it … 'I'll make the decision to leave, you won't force me out with your unending spiderweb of administration.'

So, I found myself in various offices, engaging with officials, imploring them with polite stubbornness to help me get that stamp, and demonstrating an unyielding readiness to do whatever it took to see the process through. It became evident to them that I was not one to give up easily. I was there to stay until we found a way forward. Consequently, I spent countless hours in waiting rooms seeking the green tick or stamp and directions to the next office. When I heard '*no*', I suddenly could not speak one word of Italian and sat there not hearing anything, smiling like a simpleton until that '*no*' changed into the thud of a stamp just to get rid of me.

This determination and tenacity paid off, turning what could have been an insurmountable barrier into a stepping stone towards achieving my goal. It underscored the importance of resilience and the willingness to smile and work with local authorities to navigate the complexities of the system. Slowly and gradually, all the boxes kept getting ticked. This is done, that is done, and so on and so forth. And finally, just six weeks after moving to Italy, I was granted permanent residency.

You'll have heard of a DINK – 'Double Income No Kids'. Well, let me introduce you to a new one. It's called NINK, meaning 'No Income No Kids'. Whatever little savings I had prior to coming here have been slowly whittled away. I don't want to be a NINK. I want to be a SINK – 'Single Income No Kids'. Developing a steady source of income is one of my top priorities at the moment, and my Academy alone is not going to cut it – pay the groceries, yes … more, no. I hope this shows the other side of the picture, where everything is not as bright as it seems. More on this later.

When writing this chapter, my first Italian winter is around the corner. I've even heard some expats talking about how winters here can be quite challenging, which I believe I am not completely ready for. But then again, being from the UK and Ireland, I can handle my fair share of cold, wet and rain.

Life inherently comprises turbulence and trials, each of us carrying our own burdens. However, this reality doesn't preclude us from seeking improvement, maintaining an optimistic perspective and consistently finding the silver lining in every cloud. Speaking from personal experience, having navigated the dark waters of depression and coming to understand the profound importance of finding joy in the small things, I understand the power of perseverance and positivity. I encourage you to do the same. Approach life with positivity. Your life doesn't require painstaking plans and detail, but if it is grounded in positivity regardless of your circumstances, then you'll make the best of the hand you've been dealt. A simple glance upwards at the brilliant blue sky, feeling the sun's warmth, fills my heart with a profound sense of peace and fulfilment that I've been looking for. In embracing this positive mindset, I find not just contentment but also a powerful drive to continue forging on, no matter what lies ahead.

It's crucial though to recognise that it isn't merely your own actions shaping your future. The individuals who surround you play a pivotal role in defining your life. Choosing your path wisely, considering both your destination and the characters you'll encounter along the way, is of utmost importance. In my experience, I've been luckier than I ever dared to hope, with both people and places.

Embracing change has been profoundly uplifting, providing me with a fresh outlook and an invigorated passion for life. Take, for example, my post-work ritual. Each day, when finished teaching, I find myself in a local café that's alive with a bustling crowd. The place is a melting pot of generations, with children's laughter mixed in with the wisdom of the elderly – I think, as I haven't the foggiest notion what they are saying. Individuals from every walk of life come together, creating an irresistibly vibrant atmosphere. I make it a point to stop by, treating myself to a bottle of beer in the sun. It's there, amidst the lively chatter and the comings and goings of locals, that I immerse myself in the local culture and camaraderie. Engaging with the Montaionese, sharing moments of genuine connection and then making my way home has become a cherished part of my day. It's these simple pleasures that enrich my life here.

In Montaione, the sense of community is so strong that anonymity is impossible. Everyone knows everyone – their family, their cousins, their grandparents, their dog's name. So, apparently, everyone is familiar with who I am – my endeavours and my ongoing slow journey to speak Italian. One evening, as I sat in a bar enjoying my beer, a plate of food unexpectedly landed on my table. I explained in broken Italian that I was sorry, but I hadn't order anything. To my surprise, I was told that the meal was complimentary. The owner of the bar, aware that I was a single British/Irish man in his mid-50s – no doubt useless at feeding himself – had sent me down a plate of food for dinner. She was right, cooking is not among my regular activities. My attempt to pay was then refused. This thoughtful gesture, based on a keen observation, couldn't help but bring a smile to my face. It's these small acts of kindness and the warmth of the community that truly enrich my life here. When I went there the next time, I was greeted with another plate of food … Tuscany is like a kind mother who's feeding me. Just because they know I won't be cooking for myself, they have taken the liberty to ensure I don't go to bed on an empty stomach – a lovely kind gesture.

Trying to learn Italian at my age is sometimes beautiful, sometimes a disaster. Occasionally, I wake up feeling utterly invincible, brimming with the conviction that today I will be mistaken for a local: 'Where did Barry the English teacher go? All I see is Barriano.' This soaring confidence often meets a swift reality check once I'm at the office, stationed behind my desk. The scenario typically unfolds with someone entering and launching into a stream of Italian, each word of which sails right over my head. It's in these instances that I'm struck by a sobering realisation: I haven't the foggiest notion what they're saying, and I'll never get it. I am then thrown from the lofty heights of fluency back to the humbling position of a toddler not having the first notion about what is happening.

Resigned to my linguistic crapness, I revert to my all-too-familiar refrain: *Mi dispiace, non capisco l'italiano. Parla inglese?* Thus begins our elaborate ballet of communication, a dance of hands and gestures as we strive to bridge the linguistic divide. Resorting to Google Translate on my phone, we painstakingly piece together understanding, albeit at the expense of my pride and a sliver of dignity. The ensuing disappointment is palpable, a sentiment only slightly alleviated by my phone that spares me from total mortification.

The realisation that my grasp of Italian falls short of my aspirations is, without a doubt, disheartening. Each episode serves as a poignant reminder of my age and fat tongue – a challenge that, despite its recurrent nature, never fails to sting. On the bright side, my students are absolutely delighted to have a native English speaker as their teacher. I'm teaching them conversational English and the whole notion is working well.

It was in between these Italian-learning highs and lows that one night, while I was driving back home, I experienced a milestone. I was listening to Italian radio, trying to learn new words and picking out the very few I already knew. Usually, I'll hear a word, register it and then translate it. This time, though, I heard them say *ventidue.* It means twenty-two. The moment it was said, it didn't need to be processed or translated. It was spontaneous in my head – twenty-two. Seems minor as I write it, but not having to send it through my rusty cogs was a significant moment for me. A very rare one too. If you're learning a language, just hang in there and try not to be too upset with yourself when you haven't a clue. Apparently, it gets better.

As I've mentioned previously, beyond the various challenges and adventures, it is the people that truly make all the difference. In my experience, the locals have been nothing short of extraordinary. Despite being an outsider, which could understandably lead to a somewhat frosty reception, I have encountered nothing but warmth and kindness. The people here exemplify patience, kindness and, most crucially, acceptance. I also believe, though, that you have to immerse yourself with the locals. You must have the right attitude and approach. It's imperative to venture out, engage with the community and reciprocate the warmth and hospitality shown by them. Secluding yourself, only venturing out sporadically to the nearest supermarket when you need bread or milk, isn't sufficient to forge meaningful connections or to witness the best of what the locals have to offer. Building relationships is a collaborative endeavour.

My current key to successfully living abroad is to take on that task and immerse myself in the community as much as possible. This is achieved through various means, such as joining local clubs or societies, attending dance classes or participating in community events that offer opportunities for interaction. I also took the initiative to join a walking group, which turned out to be an excellent decision.

We spent four hours trekking through the breathtaking countryside, surrounded by scenic beauty. The experience of sharing these moments with welcoming individuals was truly remarkable. It offered a profound insight into their hospitality, enriching my understanding and appreciation of the community. Engaging in such activities not only enhances the living abroad experience, but also cements a deeper connection with the local way of life. Not a word was understood between us, but we seemed to enjoy each other's company, nonetheless.

I was even invited by one of my students to their house for lunch. It was an amazing experience to sit with them, trying to communicate in my broken Italian and their broken English. We laughed together from the start of the meal to the end, a wonderful afternoon. You have to try. It would be easy to envelop yourself within an expat community. That has never been for me. I moved to a foreign culture and land to be surrounded by the foreign culture, not to be spending my time with British and Irish neighbours. If you present yourself as a recluse, that's how you will be treated no matter where you are. But if you treat that place like your home and the people as your family, they too will try their best to make you feel at home. If you ask me, I have had no qualms whatsoever about putting myself around, although you do need a bit of a brass neck at times – and don't be shy to fail again and again and again.

There are many reasons why I chose Italy, and specifically Tuscany, to call home. Let's start with the architecture, which is historic and stunningly beautiful. Next, the Tuscan people are friendly, welcoming, patient and make me feel right at home. Tuscany is also the birthplace of the Renaissance and some of history's greatest artists, such as Michelangelo, Puccini and Leonardo da Vinci. In my opinion, any region that can produce such wonderful artists has to be something special. Then there's the weather, one of my favourite factors. And it's not just the sun – there are also apocalyptic thunderstorms that rattle your bones from time to time and end just as suddenly as they begin. There are storms that make you think, 'so this is how the world ends,' and an hour later, the sun is shining, and everything feels washed and renewed. Then we move to food, which I have no words to define. It's the best in the world – sorry, France, but Italy does it way better. The same goes for the wine. I am not much of a drinker, but the wine here is simply irresistible – it helps that it is grown on the far side of my terrace. When I first arrived in Montaione in 2015 as a tourist, I knew that this was precisely what and where I had been looking for. That was nearly 10 years ago, and my opinion hasn't wavered since that first visit. In fact, it has been confirmed and strengthened.

Chapter 10
A, E, I, O, U and Don't Fear Fear

The 5th of October 2023 has marked a milestone in my journey, as I am now a permanent resident of Italy. These past six weeks, I've been jumping through hoops – it's certainly felt like a lengthy ordeal getting to this point. I had been travelling on my EU passport, but there are many obstacles if you do not possess actual residency – such as buying a car or making use of the Italian healthcare service among others. You must be a resident to do this regardless of EU status. I've had a visit from the local police and have had to go through multiple applications and office visits, but it is finally done. Now all I need to do is wait for five years and I can apply for an Italian passport and travel as an Italian – if I so wish.

My next hurdle is the language. I practise my Italian every day, discovering new things about the language. It is a blessing for me to be learning Italian as an adult, rather than learning English as an adult. Take a look at vowels – A, E, I, O, U. Everyone who speaks English knows them and how to pronounce them. Did you know that in English we actually pronounce them in 21 different ways?

Take the vowel E, for example. In the word 'each', we pronounce the 'e' as 'ee', whereas, in the word 'leg', it is more of an 'a'. So, in different words, we are pronouncing them differently. Whereas in Italian, the A, E, I, O and U are all pronounced the same way in every single word. Yes, there are a few very minor exceptions, but to my novice ears, there is no difference in the slightest. So, if you are pronouncing a word in Italian containing a vowel, it sounds the same in every other word containing the same vowel. This is one aspect of learning Italian that I found to be convenient.

Since coming here in August, I have mostly been on my own in real terms. I have no partner, no children here, no family or close friends. It was this solitude that prompted a TikTok follower to ask if

I was lonely. It got me thinking – am I lonely or merely just alone? I thought for a few days and concluded that, although I was alone, I was by no means lonely. I accept that on occasions I would quite like to turn and say to someone 'Look at that – isn't it beautiful? (or funny, or strange)' or 'Listen to that sound – isn't it gorgeous?' But for the most part, I am able to fit into my own skin and my own head. It is solitude, yes, and I am content in it for the moment. I am fine and happy. I have seen and known people in apparently strong relationships who were extremely lonely. I have also known individuals who even when surrounded by others often feel alone. I include myself in this.

If I were to condense it, it all comes down to how you are feeling, what you seek, and what you have. In my case, I've come to Italy seeking nothing but the sun and clear blue skies. Slowly and gradually, things are starting to fall into place. Where I am, and how I am, I am absolutely loving it – content, happy, smiling and satisfied. But would I like to be alone forever? No, I don't want that. I will just let nature take its course and see where it takes me. I am in no rush. I believe that, so far, I have been in love four times in my life and heartbroken once through my own choosing. I am a hopeless romantic but, at 53, will I have another take-my-breath-away love left in me? Right now, it all seems like too much trouble – especially at my age. Perhaps it is my half-a-century of experience being alive on this planet, having had some partners and observing people carefully that has led me to escape the drama and appreciate the serenity and calmness that Tuscany offers me. Perhaps a fresh pastry with a curl-your-toes cup of coffee is all the company I need for now. In time to come, I may have someone to share the tranquillity of Tuscany with, a friend or perhaps even someone close to me, but at the moment I'm not searching. For now, I'll see where this journey takes me, allow events to unfold in their own time and let love find its way. It may be a combination of those thoughts and something magical about this place that, every morning, I find myself waking up with a bright, beaming smile, throwing my legs out of the side of the bed and saying, 'Bring it on.'

I have already mentioned that prior to moving, in the planning stage, I had to come up with an idea that would give me an income. I decided to stick to one of my strengths, which is my ability to speak and comprehend English fluently. I'm a native, so I am obviously well versed, making it my strength. I decided to teach English, seeing as how it's the universal language, and more and more people are inclined towards learning it nowadays. But that was not going to be enough. I had to build on the foundation and create a fortified structure, i.e. credentials, certifications.

So, I had to research it, study it and take exams. TEFL (Teaching English as a Foreign Language) and TESOL (Teaching English to Speakers of Other Languages) certified – tick. I have the certificates displayed on my wall at the Academy. Thus, my 'potential' (and I stress potential) source of income was established – the little Toscana English Academy. I mean it's no bigger than my previous bathroom, but hey, it works for me. I advertised a little and, lo and behold, a few students enrolled to learn English.

Aside from teaching face-to-face, there is also the option of teaching online. I haven't taken the plunge yet as most of my research suggests that you teach throughout the night to Asian students and get paid very little for it.

It all comes down to skill and graft. Nowadays, there are a myriad of skills that can help you earn a decent income remotely. I recommend going on websites like indeed.com and searching for remote jobs. If you find the right job that compliments your skills, you could be sitting in France, Australia, USA or in Tuscany, working remotely to earn some money. But a skill is a must, and not having one is a pitfall for anyone looking to make the move with no proper plan.

Being an online security adviser appears to be popular with digital nomads, but that's not my thing. You need to have something to offer

If you are a native English speaker, you can acquire the said certifications and become an English teacher in a small town or online. Simply acquire a small space – this could be at home – that you can transform into your personal classroom, and start with that. It's not as difficult as it seems but, at the same time, take it too lightly and it won't work. If you do it right, it will buy your groceries, but it will not put you on any rich list.

I have mentioned before that when I left home in the late 1980s, aged 17, I had to queue up every Sunday night outside the telephone box to speak to my mum and dad. The world has drastically transformed now, thanks to technology, making connection easy and convenient. It is unrecognisable from when I was a child. I can talk to my children whenever I want. We have FaceTime, WhatsApp, Messenger and all kinds of apps on our smartphones that make it easy for us to stay in touch. We can send messages and pictures in seconds. You can directly videocall anyone anywhere in the world. With conference calls, it's like all of us are sitting in the same room. This is one aspect that makes the idea of moving abroad way more acceptable to many.

Then there are local factors, such as cultural differences, but even that gap has been reduced. I am getting the same television, radio and internet as I was when I was in the UK and Ireland. If I want, I can watch all the shows that are being watched back home. I don't but, if I wanted to, I could, as it's all here. I do like football, so I watch Sky Sports. If you are emigrating, you no longer feel as if you're being transported to the moon.

It doesn't matter where you are, the world is much smaller than ever before, not to mention convenient. In my case, I have the option of being as much British or Irish as I want to be, or I can be as much Italian as I want. But for me, the latter is better here, so I am more biased toward that. Since I am in the process of learning the language, it is only natural for me to be more inclined towards Italian radio and TV, although quality is an issue. Whenever I turn on and try to watch

Italian TV, I appear to be met with a central male host, a screaming audience, a large spinning wheel and a woman standing in the centre of the screen wearing only a bikini. But the most significant difference about being in Italy – apart from your friends and family not being right on your doorstep – is the weather.

If you do fancy taking the plunge, or at least looking into it, you must do a bit of research. Research the people, culture, language and way of life wherever you are thinking of going. What is the point of going somewhere if you detest the food, the people and the culture? What's the point of going to a place where you are not sure of your own safety – where you are always looking over your shoulder, scared that someone might follow you home if you are a female? In the end, choose to go wherever your heart desires, but be informed. You could even try it out for a few months first. But always remember, being a money-spending tourist during the summer is very different to being a 365 permanent resident who needs an income to live.

For me, it was not that difficult a decision. Choosing Italy was rather simple. I had been coming here for years, so I knew the area. In fact, I already had a property in Tuscany that I had purchased in 2016. I loved the natural beauty of the region, along with the art, food, culture and the people … it all collectively pulls you in.

I have had people write to me and say they would be too scared or too afraid to do what I have done. If you are thinking about emigrating, you need to change the perception you have regarding moving abroad and starting your life over, and, more importantly, you need to change your vocabulary and eliminate the words 'scared' or 'afraid'. Just get rid of them altogether.

If you think something like this will make you feel scared, or will frighten you, write that word on a piece of paper and change words such as 'fear' or 'scared' to 'concern'. Making such a move would give you cause for concern. The word 'fear' is a powerful word that has been programmed to strike unease in our hearts since our childhood. The word will always make you run away from whatever it is that you are trying to face. It will prevent you from achieving new things or having new experiences because, in the end, you will be too afraid to do it.

On the other hand, 'concern' is a comparatively positive term that prompts a different kind of reaction. For most individuals, it prompts curiosity, discovery and a willingness to resolve the problem at hand. Words such as 'fear' and 'afraid' will make you feel out of your comfort zone. But it is only by stepping out of your comfort zone that you will truly grow. Instead of saying 'I am scared of moving to Italy', say 'I am concerned about moving to Italy'. Notice the difference? It is very natural to be concerned when making such a major move, but, at the same time, the word prompts you to face the problem head-on and try to find a solution. What solution can you find to alleviate this concern that you have? Instead of automatically saying 'no', you have put your thinking hat on and are now coming up with solutions.

Even if you have rational reasons that might keep you grounded – such as finances, children, grandchildren, etc. – you have still conquered your fear and have rid yourself of a negative emotion, and a powerful one at that. Just don't let fear ever hold you back from doing anything. And it doesn't just apply to when you are looking to emigrate to another country. It can also apply to other situations in life. Just get rid of these crippling negative words and change them to concern, a positive and empowering word that will enable you to come up with a solution. For all you know, this is the push you need to sort out your affairs and prepare for a future of solutions.

Chapter 11
Festivals and Reflection

October in Tuscany is harvest season: come the harvest, come the festivals – wonderful. The food festivals here are a food lover's dream come true. October brings the truffle, cheese, mushroom, chocolate, nougat, olive oil and apple festivals. But it doesn't stop there. There are also celebrations dedicated to wild game, wild boar, chestnuts, Christmas cake, hot sauces, honey and breads. It's clear that autumn in Italy is a season of culinary delights, offering more than just a taste of local culture. It's a time when every bite tells a story, every festival a chapter of Italian tradition. Italy in the harvest season is a reminder that life is delicious and that happiness can be found in the most unexpected of flavours.

During festivals the streets are lined with tables groaning under the weight of delicious foods. For someone who loves food as much as I do, this is pretty much paradise. I might have missed mentioning a few festivals here and there, but these are the ones that captured my imagination and taste buds. It's a whirlwind of flavours and experiences that I love, and I'm keen to dive into them again year upon year.

Life here at the moment is punctuated by days of sunshine and days of storms. I have and will share tales of days filled with joy, remarkable experiences and extraordinary individuals. Yet it's crucial to acknowledge that not every day is puppy dogs and rainbows. There are rare periods of gloom, where an unseen force seems to siphon away all vitality. Living with depression has taught me that storm clouds pass; these moments demand patience and resilience. Believe me, it is 100 times easier dealing with those days when the skies are a brilliant blue, the sun lightens your environment and the heat warms your skin.

At the seasoned age of 53, I find myself to be a reasonably

emotionally scarred individual – not any more than most, just testimony to a life richly lived. By this stage in life, if you haven't accumulated a collection of emotional scars, you've been living in a cave. Being a positive person, I've nurtured a streak of optimism throughout most of my life. But when it comes to the existence of the soul, the spirit and an aura, I'm a major Doubting Thomas. These concepts never quite resonated with me. Yet, in this moment, if such an inner soul or spirit does exist, I've brushed against something akin to perfection and happiness, a sensation unparalleled in what I've experienced before. There's a voice within, perhaps long silenced, shouting that I've finally found where I belong … 'You've found your tribe – about bloody time.'

Through my life, it's these moments of profound introspection and connection that sculpt my understanding of existence, peace and happiness. Through my online connections, I see that there's an enormous number of people hungering not just for a change of scenery but for a whole new chapter in their lives. They dream of casting off the constraints we often impose on ourselves. The desire to step out into the world and chase those dreams is powerful and widespread. Taking the leap towards living those dreams is more about planning and less about the daunting financial aspects that many fear. It's not merely about the money – though, naturally, finances play a significant role. The real task is in the preparation: work out where you want to go, calculate your potential living costs, figure out if your skills can earn you enough not just to survive, but thrive.

The good news is that we live in a connected world where there are ample resources to help dreamers realise their dream. From the reactions I've seen, it's clear my jump has ignited a spark in some. I've been asked, many times, for advice about making such a move, and I'm happy to provide that. I'm more than ready to offer advice and support. I'm happy to be the stepping stone for someone's leap into their dream life. It's understandable that not everyone has the courage to take that first step alone, which is precisely why I'm happy to help with advice.

I'm convinced that anyone who visits Tuscany will fall head over heels for this place – its beauty, its people and, without a doubt, its incredible food. If you fancy investigating the possibility of living abroad, research thoroughly what the place is like 12 months a year, not just in high-tourist season. Tuscany is a very different place in January than it is in August. Before the move, even contemplate spending a month in your dream location and shop where the locals shop, eat what the locals eat and do what the locals do. You might change your mind, or you might reinforce the idea that it's what you want.

The beauty of Tuscany doesn't stop at its landscapes. The region's passion for festivals and celebrations adds another layer to its charm. Observing the local community embrace the spirit of each festivity, from the quirky and unique to the traditional, fills me with an immense sense of gratitude for the opportunity to be part of this vibrant culture. The streets of Tuscany transform into a canvas, displaying everything from meticulously tended gardens to elusive art installations tucked away in hidden corners. This sense of discovery is what makes every outing an adventure, akin to a treasure hunt where the prizes are the breathtaking artworks and experiences that wait around every corner. The more I explore, the more I realise that this place never ceases to amaze, offering endless treasures for those willing to look.

After navigating through multiple autumnal festivals and soaking up invaluable lessons along the way, I have noticed that late November's arrival has marked a transition, hinting at changes ahead. The weather can change dramatically. Zz The storms here aren't like anything I've ever experienced before. They are almost apocalyptic displays of lightning, rain and thunder. They arrive, display and disappear almost as quickly. I turn everything off, open the shutters and windows and marvel at the performance. Despite the occasional theatrical display by the weather in November and December, the climate here has remained, for the most part, surprisingly mild. But 'this is not normal' the locals tell me.

Wandering through the experiences Tuscany offers, from the charm of its festivals to the embrace of its unpredictable weather, has been a journey of discovery and appreciation. Being here has taught me, and is teaching me, the value of finding joy and contentment in the moment, whether it's in the wonder of a festival, the peace of a quiet sunny day, or the spectacle of a theatrical storm. It's a reminder of the beauty in diversity and the joy of simple pleasures – a story that enriches not just the mind but also the soul.

Chapter 12
Immersion, the Mayor and Tinkerbell

Embarking on a journey to set roots in Tuscany is filled with both anticipation and introspection. The notion of relocating to such a storied region often stirs a deep yearning for a connection to its rich cultural heritage and breathtaking landscapes. Yet the path to making this dream a reality is layered with practicalities and personal reflections that extend beyond mere logistics.

In my own quest for a home in Tuscany, the process was not just about finding a place to live; it was a profound journey of self-discovery and adaptation. The initial excitement of exploring potential homes was tempered by the realisation of the financial and emotional investments required. It's about more than just good savings and energy; it demands a resilience and readiness to immerse into a new way of life.

Choosing the right location was pivotal. The allure of northern Italy, specifically Verona, was undeniable, yet practical considerations like budget constraints guided my decision-making process. The desire to be near an airport, for instance, wasn't just a logistical preference but a reflection of my need to remain connected to the world beyond Tuscany's rolling hills.

The criteria for my ideal property evolved into a reflection of my lifestyle preferences and priorities. Opting for a home with a maintenance fee wasn't merely a convenience; it was a conscious choice to prioritise leisure and enjoyment of the Tuscan experience over the burdens of upkeep. I wanted somewhere within a complex where I paid a maintenance charge and a professional company looked after everything outside my door.

Navigating the intricacies of the Italian real estate and legal systems was another layer of complexity. The role of a bilingual notary became one of not just a legal expert but also a crucial guide through the unfamiliar terrain of legal procedures, being the bridge between my aspirations and the realisation of my Tuscan dream. The interaction with the state functioning notary underscored the solemnity of the commitment I was making, not only to the property but to a new chapter of my life in Italy.

Buying property in a foreign country is a daunting task. The intricate details, the unfamiliar legal landscapes and the sheer volume of paperwork can easily overwhelm even the most determined of spirits. This is where the value of experienced professionals comes into play. Enlisting the help of estate agents, legal experts and other specialists not only alleviates much of the stress involved but also ensures that every step of the process is handled with precision and care. But beware – they know how to charge. Maintaining open lines of communication with your team is crucial. Regular updates can provide peace of mind and help to pre-empt any potential issues before they become problematic.

The transformative experience of settling in Italy, for me, has been nothing short of extraordinary. Each day is enriching, a lifestyle that beckons people to this vibrant country. From the moment the morning sun casts its first rays, there's an undeniable energy that sweeps through the air, igniting a passion for life that is both invigorating and inspiring.

My mornings are marked by simple yet profound pleasures – the ritual of savouring a perfectly brewed cappuccino paired with a sweet pastry, a daily indulgence that somehow never tires. It's these moments of pure bliss that make the earlier challenges of relocation seem like distant memories. Interestingly, despite this daily treat, I've found myself in better shape than ever before. Perhaps it's the combination of fresh, quality ingredients and the outdoor Italian way of life that promotes a healthy balance.

The culinary landscape here is a constant revelation. Italy's food culture, known for its diversity and richness, continues to amaze me. Having always had an appreciation for fine dining, I anticipated that moving here might be a challenge for my waistline. Yet, the reality has been pleasantly surprising. The food, bursting with freshness and flavour, somehow supports a lifestyle that feels both indulgent and balanced.

Italy's gastronomic excellence is not merely about the food itself but the culture that surrounds it. Meals are more than fuel here; they are a celebration of life, the joy of sharing and a homage to the art of cooking. This deep-rooted culinary tradition has been an endless source of fascination for me, offering daily discoveries that enrich my understanding and appreciation of Italian food.

In sum, the initial complexities of purchasing a property and settling in Italy pale in comparison to the experiences that life here offers. The sun-drenched days, the exquisite food and the vibrant culture have not only fulfilled my expectations but also added a depth of flavour to my life that I hadn't anticipated. It's a journey of transformation that I relish every day, a reminder of the beauty of taking a chance.

You might wonder, as I've uprooted my whole life, have I also left work behind and retired? Not at all. I'm still very much in the working world, and I wouldn't have it any other way. Working is something I thrive on. I'm one of those people who, quite happily, will drop at my desk. The key for me has always been choosing work that I love, ensuring that every day feels more like a pursuit of interest than a chore.

Currently, I'm in the midst of pushing the new venture, the Toscana English Academy. It's an exciting phase, setting everything up and thinking of the potential it holds. Success here means more than just achievement; it's a stepping stone. I've got a couple of other business ideas simmering away, and, once the Academy is firmly on its feet, I plan to dive into these projects. It's a time of great momentum and ambition. It's all systems go from here. A new chapter in Italy is unfolding. I'm reinvesting in my future. It's a cycle of growth and investment, a belief that when one door opens, you sprint through it and fling open even more. There's much to do and endless possibilities to explore.

This is a place that is easy to fall in love with, where every street and every corner speaks of centuries of history. The best part is, they do their very best to preserve it. I absolutely love how the Tuscans are proud of their heritage, and the local government is always taking steps to ensure even the very streets are kept in their best shape.

I know there are many people who would love to come and visit here. I recently shared an idea on TikTok about offering an immersive experience of La Dolce Vita right here in Tuscany, mirroring my own journey in this beautiful place. The response was overwhelming, with many expressing a keen interest in this unique adventure. Motivated by this enthusiasm, I came up with an idea that I could formalise this concept into a quality experience, designed to bring viewers and readers into the heart of Tuscany for a seven-day, all-inclusive journey.

Here's what I came up with, anyone heading this way will start with arrival at either Pisa or Florence Airport, where I'll personally welcome them. From there, we'll dive into Tuscany, exploring renowned gems like Pisa, Florence, Peccioli, Lajatico and San Gimignano. But it's not just about the places; it's about embracing the lifestyle. The visitors' stay will include all meals and accommodation, ensuring a seamless experience.

The essence of Tuscany isn't just in its vistas but in its activities. Imagine starting your day with yoga amidst the rolling hills, spending afternoons on horseback or savouring the local wines, and evenings enjoying *aperitivi* as the sun dips below the horizon. Of course, there will be ample time for relaxation by the pool, basking in the Tuscan sun. I want to make this more than just a vacation; it will be an invitation to experience, learn and indulge in the beauty of Tuscany. At the time of writing, I'm at the planning stage and I hope to get it up and running and welcome some of you to this beautiful part of the world. After all, it is about immersing yourself and integrating in the community and being a part of it.

In my journey to integrate into the local community here, I've not only joined groups but also embraced the unique opportunity to grow and learn from each experience. Participating in the local football team's games, for instance, has offered me more than just entertainment. It's provided a sense of belonging and an insider's view into the passions that unite this community. Watching a game alongside locals, cheering and sharing in their excitement, I've learned the value of sport as a universal language, capable of bridging gaps even when words fail.

For anyone looking to make the most out of living in a new country, I've learned that stepping out of your comfort zone and engaging with the community is key. It's through these engagements that you find not just a sense of belonging but also a deeper appreciation for the community. In return, the community will accept you back. I am living proof of that.

Some time ago, I had the honour of receiving a personal letter from the *Sindaco*, or Mayor, of Montaione. It was a warm welcome, extending his and the people of his community's hospitality and support for me and my new venture here. The mayor, representing the community, assured me that they were eager to assist in any way possible. This gesture is an example of the incredible warmth and generosity I've encountered since my arrival.

The people of Montaione are genuinely kind-hearted. Their willingness to help – whether it's offering a hand with home improvements, assisting with language barriers or simply showing patience as I navigate through learning Italian – has been overwhelming. Their support is not just a mere formality; it's a deeply ingrained part of their community spirit.

This experience has revealed a profound truth about integrating into a new community. It's not just about the acknowledgement or assistance you receive on the surface, but more about the deeper connections and mutual respect that develops. Being welcomed by the mayor, and the people of Montaione, has shown me that the essence of belonging lies in reciprocal appreciation and contribution. I've come to realise that my journey here is not just about finding my place in Tuscany, but also about how I can contribute to the fabric of this community. The privilege isn't just Montaione's acceptance of me, as the mayor wrote in his letter; it's my opportunity to be a part of something larger than myself. It's a reminder that we all seek connection and purpose, and through giving back, we find our true place in the world.

As I reflect on this chapter of my life, the wisdom I've gleaned is clear: belonging and fulfilment come from embracing the community with an open heart and a willingness to contribute. In doing so, we enrich not only our own lives but hopefully also the lives of those around us. It's a beautiful cycle of support and growth that I'm eager to be a part of. My hope is to be as much of an asset to Montaione as they have been to me, fostering a legacy of mutual respect and shared growth.

Since moving here, I've developed an aspiration, a quest, to acquire a Vespa. I haven't the foggiest notion where this came from – my fascination with them is somewhat inexplicable. Never before have I mounted a Vespa. In fact, I've never been on a motorbike/scooter, ever. Yet the thought of cruising through Tuscany, the birthplace of the Vespa, instilled in me a sense of unbridled joy. I started looking for a small Vespa/scooter for what I wanted – simply to commute back and forward to work and mosey to the shops – but the prices for these scooters were simply unjustifiable.

I occasionally employ someone as a very capable handyman, Taku. He doesn't speak English and I've no Italian, but we get along and have a laugh using WhatsApp and iPhone translations. He is fabulous when I need him for all sorts of jobs, so he gets the occasional bottle of Bushmills Irish whiskey as an additional thank you. A day or two after the last job he did for me, he sent me a message on WhatsApp asking if I was still looking for a scooter. I said I was, so he asked me to meet him in a town some 20 minutes from my home. When I arrived, he introduced me to a work colleague and showed me a scooter. It looked in good enough condition, so I prepped myself for negotiation. I asked the price, and he said, 'Nothing, free. You are a friend of Taku, and I know you will look after this scooter.' Incredible. He insisted against my protests that no payment was necessary for someone who would value and care for it as much as I would.

Today such generosity is rare, and this is evidence of the remarkable community spirit I have found in this part of the world. It's moments like these that truly define the warmth and hospitality of Tuscany, turning simple acts of kindness into memories that will last a lifetime. And yes, riding a scooter through the Tuscan countryside in the sun is as amazing and wonderful as I'd hoped it would be. I've named the scooter Tinkerbell – small but powerful.

Above: The Toscana English Academy today.

Top Right: My son and Italian friends Daniela and Stefano enjoying dinner in Montaione.

Below: A view in Cinque Terre.

Below: Tuscany is famous for Fiorentine steaks – wonderful.

Below: My wonderful dad and amazing children, Christmas 2023.

Above: Getting involved with the Italian culture without a word of Italian.

Bottom right: At the annual truffle festival in my home town.

Below: The view from my home.

Above and above right: The amazing Concorde.

Right: The doors in Italy are stunning. I love them.

Below: A small village chapel ceiling.

Below right: The wonderful hospitality of Podere la Casetta, Montaione.

Above left: Some of my guests enjoying yoga with Claudia.

Above: Lunch on my terrace.

Below left: Alberto Bocelli (Andrea's brother) at the family restaurant.

Below: Elle from Carpe Diem showing us how to cook.

Chapter 13
Importance of Coffee and Shedding the Toot

As the dawn of a new day unfolds, my journey through the intricacies of Italian coffee begins. It has become a habitual routine, and I love it. Coffee, a simple pleasure that Italy holds dear, boasts a diversity that is as rich and as varied as the country's own history. The Italians, known for their passionate love affair with *un caffè*, have perfected the art of coffee-making, crafting an array of concoctions that can delight or dismay, depending on your palate. I've had the privilege of sampling an array of these creations, each with its own character. Let us delve into the heart of Italian coffee culture and explore some of the flavours it offers.

The cappuccino takes its name from the Capuchin friars, its colour reminiscent of their robes, a harmonious blend of espresso, milk and foam, creating a comfort in a cup that warms the soul. Then there's the espresso, the quintessential Italian brew – intense, rich and potent – and by far the most popular drink in Italy. The *caffè mocha*, or mocha coffee, introduces a luxurious twist, marrying espresso with chocolate and steamed milk – pure indulgence.

An adventure in flavour, the *affogato*, marries espresso's warmth with the cool sweetness of ice cream, creating a mix as delightful as it is unexpected. The *caffè freddo* offers a brisk refreshment, though its chilled nature might not cater to all tastes. With the *caffè lungo*, or long coffee, boiling water dilutes the intensity of espresso, offering a milder, longer experience.

For those seeking a spirited kick, the *caffè corretto* 'corrects' an espresso with a dash of liquor, a bold blend that challenges the senses. The *americano*, a lighter affair, waters down espresso to suit a palate craving gentleness. The *macchiato*, with its 'stain' of milk, provides a subtle softness to the robust espresso base.

The *caffè con panna*, espresso crowned with cream, offers a decadent escape, while the *caffè ristretto*, a restricted coffee, concentrates the essence of espresso into a potent shot, electrifying the senses. The double espresso, or *caffè doppio*, doubles the pleasure with a robust intensity, while the *caffè con schiuma*, coffee with foam, adds a light, airy touch to the rich espresso foundation.

Having travelled on this sensory journey through Italy's coffee, I've encountered flavours ranging from the complex to the delightfully simple. Coffee remains not just a drink but a celebration of flavour, craftsmanship and tradition. It stands as evidence to Italy's culinary excellence, a symphony of tastes that delights the senses, invites contemplation and, above all, brings joy to those who drink it in its countless forms. Not to mention that a visit for coffee adds another level of social connection to the many locals who drop in, have a quick conversation and *un caffè* in the *tabacchi* during the day.

Having consumed it almost every morning, I stand, at times, before my gas hob, fancying myself gradually mastering the art of coffee brewing. With ritualistic patience, I'll watch the coffee simmer – a growing skill I'm quietly getting proud of. My approach to coffee is simple. I enjoy it warm and straightforward, without fussing over whether it is strong or weak. It was this unpretentious love for coffee that led me to a moment of unexpected vulnerability. Eager to test my new coffee skills, I decided to offer a cup of my brew to an Italian workman who had come to assess some work in my apartment. This wasn't just any coffee, but a cup bearing the weight of my novice pride. Without revealing my intentions, I silently hoped using him as a guinea pig would confirm my coffee-making credentials. I was half expecting to get a Paul Hollywood-style handshake and a 'welcome to Italy, my Italian friend'. His reaction, however, was a lesson wrapped in silence. Without uttering a single word, he made this god-awful screwed up face and simply placed the cup down after a single taste and proceeded to discuss the job at hand. His unspoken verdict was a mirror reflecting my premature confidence back at me, leaving me to confront the deep divide between enthusiasm and expertise. I was crestfallen, a mix of embarrassment and a newfound humility washing over me. In his restraint – for he neither spat nor vomited – despite what his expression hinted at, I found a poignant reminder of further work needing to be done.

This experience, humbling as it was, did not dampen my spirit, but rather it deepened my appreciation for the craft and the requirement for improvement. It was a reminder that the essence of growth often lies in the courage to present our efforts to the world, ready or not, and to find resilience in the face of gentle, or not so gentle, rebuke.

Recently there has been a debate unfolding here on the very essence of what makes a place ideal for calling home. This debate was about the best place to live in Italy, which was sparked by a recent survey that had pitted the northern regions against their southern counterparts in a discussion that extended beyond mere amenities and services. According to the survey, the north emerged as the premier choice for living, celebrated for its superior infrastructure, including unrivalled internet connectivity, impeccable roads and comprehensive facilities. Yet this revelation was met with extremely vocal resistance from the south.

The southern regions, with a blend of indignation and pride, raised counterarguments that delved deep into the soul of what life there had to offer. They argued that, while the north might boast advanced technological connectivity, it lacked the pristine beaches, the unrivalled freshness of local cuisine and the genuine warmth and openness of its communities. These were the aspects where the south shone, and it offered a stark contrast to the bustling, often impersonal, pace of life in the north.

What unfolded was a rich narrative that explored the depth of Italy's regional diversity, highlighting a clash not of mere preferences but of identities. The survey, while meticulously noting tangible assets like infrastructure and proximity to medical facilities, seemingly overlooked the intangible qualities that gave a place its spirit and warmth. The essence of this debate lay in understanding that Italy, with its varied regions, offered a mosaic of experiences shaped by both its people and its places.

The emotional core reflected a profound connection to the land and its culture. For those drawn to the hustle and efficiency of a more urban life, the north presented an appealing prospect, where innovation and convenience took precedence. Conversely, the south offered a sanctuary for those seeking a slow life surrounded by nature, community and the timeless rituals of traditional cuisine and hospitality, where life moved at a rhythm dictated not by the clock but by the seasons and the sea.

I can safely say I am living in a place that I will not trade for anything. Despite the uncertainty of whether the seasons and weather are being affected by climate change, the beauty of the clear blue skies is undeniable. The winter daytime brings a coolness that necessitates a coat. As we approach the end of November, temperatures hover around 15 degrees by day, but nights are a different story, often dipping close to zero. Unlike homes in the UK and Ireland, where multiple versions of insulation combat the cold, my apartment here offers no such comfort. It's built for 30+ degrees, compelling me to bundle up warmly under an electric blanket in the evenings. I've even taken to wearing a Sherlock Holmes-style bed hat to keep cosy through the chillier nights.

There's a beauty in this weather that I deeply appreciate. The joy of sunlight during the day fills me with well-being. And there's something magical about this crisp weather, with the festive season approaching. I know that around this time of year, the local town will be illuminated with Christmas lights. This blending of clear, sunny days with the onset of holiday festivities creates a backdrop that feels both vibrant and deeply comforting.

Simplicity – not just of the weather, but of life – is something that has been becoming more and more meaningful to me. The more I dive deeper into what it represents, the more it becomes evident that this is perhaps all I need – a simple yet meaningful life. So, decluttering and simplifying life has not only brought about a profound transformation that goes beyond mere location but also created a narrative of shedding the unnecessary, of finding freedom in minimalism. A vivid illustration of this transition can be found in something as mundane as the keys I carry. Once, I resembled a medieval jailer, weighed down by a jangling collection of keys that represented various compartments of my life, each tucked away in bulging pockets. Now, my keyring holds just three keys – one for my car, one for my office and one for my apartment. This simple change serves as a constant reminder of my deliberate choice to pare down to the essentials, and it's a source of genuine contentment.

This shift wasn't just about physical possessions; it was an emotional and mental cleanse. The multitude of unused items that once cluttered my space didn't just occupy my home; they burdened my mind and weighed me down. The act of decluttering wasn't merely about creating more space, but about liberating myself from the chains of material possessions. Each time I chose to part with an item was a step towards a lighter, more purposeful existence … or 'getting rid of toot', as I would often say.

Now, the environment around me reflects a mindful approach to living. Every object in my apartment has earned its place through careful consideration, not just of its utility but of its value to my life. This has instilled in me a deeper appreciation for the things I own, a sense of gratitude and respect for the space I inhabit. It's a practice that extends beyond physical belongings to how I manage my time and energy, focusing on what truly enriches my life.

The joy found in this minimalist lifestyle is profound, yet it's accompanied by a curiosity about its longevity. Will this sense of satisfaction and simplicity persist over time? This question lingers, but, for now, I relish the lightness of being that comes from this intentional way of living. Decluttering has evolved into a journey of self-discovery and intentionality, teaching me that, sometimes, the key to fulfilment lies not in what we gather, but in what we are brave enough to let go.

Life is not a straight line. The peaks represent moments of joy and happiness, and the troughs are the sad or dark times that often follow, or precede, the good ones. Without the bad, we wouldn't be able to appreciate the good, and if it were all good, life would become mundane. You shouldn't, and probably can't, have too much of either. A bit of struggle is essential.

My journey through the process of learning a language has been a compendium of small victories and moments of failures alike. There are times when the pieces seem to fall into place and Italian words and phrases jump into my mouth. Yet, at other moments, clarity dissolves into confusion, leaving me grasping for understanding, especially in the spontaneous flow of everyday conversations … *'Mi dispiace, non capisco l'italiano. Parla inglese?'*

This challenge was something I hadn't fully anticipated, especially the colloquialisms or idioms that are the heartbeat of any language. It's a reminder that language is not just a tool for communication but a bridge between worlds, offering insights into the hearts and minds of others. Whether it be the weather, language or coffee, the world we live in is intricate, complex, yet beautiful. I know for a fact that the beautiful weather that I have fallen in love with is likely to go into hibernation. The clear blue skies, which I still get to enjoy, will be overtaken by clouds, snow may cover the ground, and rain might make the mood gloomy – it's all a part of life, and we should welcome it with open arms. The same goes for my bitter awful coffee. It's not quite there yet, but it will be – it will soon be drinkable. I'll never be a barista, but I won't have an Italian making that same awful face – it makes me smile to even think about it. His face was 'that's just wrong'. It was a moment of shame, but I will be reborn from my coffee ashes and learn to make a cuppa that, if not irresistible, is at least drinkable.

Chapter 14
Maria Callas, Florence and Every Day is a Schoolday

There's a particular memory that stands out vividly from my first few months of living in Italy, which marked the celebration of a centenary – the 100th year since the birth of Maria Callas, the iconic Greek opera singer whose voice transcended the ordinary, elevating the soprano to new heights. This occasion was commemorated with an evening dedicated to her legacy, in a local theatre, a gathering that promised to rekindle the magic of her artistry within the hearts of those present.

The night was graced not only with the presence of scholars, each carrying titles that spoke of their erudition, but also with the narratives they weaved about Maria Callas. Despite the language barrier that rendered their stories into mere sounds and rhythms for me, their passion and reverence for Callas was unmistakable, bridging understanding beyond words.

The highlight, however, was the performance of a soprano whose voice seemed to channel the essence of Callas herself. It was in these moments, enveloped in the pure, emotive power of opera, that the evening found its true purpose. It transcended being an event and became a profound connection to the timeless beauty and sorrow opera encapsulates, a reminder of the universal language of music that Callas so masterfully spoke.

Celebrating Maria Callas's 100th birthday in such a setting underscored a deeper realisation: the enduring impact of a person's legacy. It was not merely about honouring the memory of a legendary artist but recognising how their contributions continue to inspire and move people across generations and geographies. As the night drew to a close, the experience lingered, a poignant reminder of the beauty and depth of human expression through music. It was a celebration of a life, of Callas's incomparable legacy, and of the art that endures beyond the confines of time and language, enriching the human experience.

Inspired by Callas, I decided to make the most of the following day. It was a serene Sunday morning, and a spontaneous decision beckoned me towards a trip, a quiet whisper promising the embrace of history and art. The destination was Florence. Upon arrival, the reality of its bustling life on a December morning quickly dispelled any notions of tranquillity I had harboured. The city, alive with the vibrancy of locals and visitors, held an energy that was both overwhelming and exhilarating.

In the heart of Florence, I found myself amidst the grandeur of the Basilica di Santa Maria Novella. Its architectural splendour, a silent narrative of the city's illustrious past, stood against the backdrop of a clear winter sky. The piazza was a place where every stone and statue whispered tales. Not far from there, the iconic tower of the Cathedral of Santa Maria watched over the city, its presence a constant reminder of Florence's enduring beauty and significance.

Wandering through the streets, I encountered the echoes of history in the Piazza della Signoria, where a reproduction of Michelangelo's *David* stands, amongst other wonderful statues. Florence, once the heart of Italy's political power and now the jewel and capital of Tuscany, unfolded before me, its every corner a chapter from a storybook of the Renaissance, where the Medici family once shaped the destiny of art and culture.

This captivating dander led me to the banks of the River Arno, its waters carving a path through the city. The Ponte Vecchio, with its unique congregation of shops clinging to the sides, offered a picturesque scene that captured the essence of Florence's charm. Yet it was here, away from the throng of the city centre, that I found a moment of reflection. Watching the people as they navigated their lives amidst such historical magnificence, I contemplated the delicate balance between preserving the past and embracing the living pulse of the present.

In this city, where every alleyway and bridge seems to hold a story,

I pondered what it meant to live the dream. Was it the pursuit of beauty, the search for knowledge, or simply the act of being amidst such history, participating in the age-old tradition of storytelling and creation? Florence, with its undeniable beauty and complex history, offered no simple answers, but instead invited me to appreciate the depth of our collective march through time. Reflecting on this experience, it became clear that the true essence of living is found in the rich mosaic of experiences that challenge, inspire and transform us.

Learning another language later in life often feels like navigating an unfamiliar river with its own set of currents and undercurrents. It's becoming my nemesis and my attempts to navigate my way around the new language have been met with a mix of enthusiasm and embarrassment, reflective not just of the complexities of language itself but of the intricate wiring of my human brain. It's as if my mind, so accustomed to the familiar pathways of my native tongue, hesitates at the threshold of this new world, uncertain and cautious.

This struggle was brought into sharp focus on a day that now lingers in my memory with a heavy dose of this embarrassment. Emerging from the Toscana English Academy, where the boundaries of language are defined, I encountered a moment that seemed to encapsulate my entire experience with learning Italian. A local woman, engaged in the simple yet arduous task of carrying a large bucket of water, became the unwitting participant in my quest to bridge the gap between my intention and my fat tongue expression.

In my mind, the words formed clearly – a polite offer of assistance that felt as natural as breathing. Yet what transpired was a ping-pong of miscommunication. Her response was a mirror to my own inadequacies in this new linguistic realm. Despite my repeated attempts, the chasm between my intended message and its reception could not be bridged. Her reply, though lost on me, left me pondering and searching for meaning, much like a toddler trying to make sense of the world around them. In my head I asked her if she needed help and her response in Italian translated to English was 'No, tomorrow is the 8th of December'.

It was a moment that seemed to underscore my outsider status, a reminder of what still lay ahead. This experience, humbling as it was, served as a poignant lesson in patience, persistence and the inherent vulnerability of stepping into a world where the familiar becomes foreign. This feeling of being a toddler, grappling with the basics of communication, is not a regression, although it does sometimes feel like it, but a necessary phase in the acquisition of new knowledge. It is a reminder that in the pursuit of understanding, we must embrace our moments of vulnerability, for they are apparently the harbingers of eventual mastery. I do however wish my comfort zone wouldn't abandon me so much. I often see it disappear up some beautiful alleyway when I go to open my mouth and attempt my new language.

Chapter 15
Italy, a Historical Perspective

I chose to move to Italy for many reasons – beauty, architecture, food, its people, the weather – but I also want to touch on the fascinating history of this wonderful country. I was surprised to know that the unification of Italy and the birth of a single nation only happened in 1861. Prior to that, Italy was a disparate collection of states being ruled by either large powerful families or nations outside the borders of what we now call Italy.

Etruscans: 900–500 BC

The Etruscans were an ancient civilisation that existed in central Italy between 900 BC and 500 BC. Their exact origins are still being debated. Some say they came from Turkey, others that they were native Italians. They were a deeply religious society but one that traded extensively (producing iron, wine, ceramics, art), owned slaves, were formidable warriors, promoted the arts and provided women with more freedom that their Roman successors. Etruscans were highly developed in terms of art and architecture, and their burial practices were elaborate, with tombs decorated with vivid frescoes depicting scenes of daily life, banquets and the afterlife. Etruscan society fell into decline in the 4th century BC with the growing power of the Romans.

Romans: 753 BC–476 AD

According to Roman mythology, Rome was founded in 753 BC by Romulus, who, along with his twin brother, Remus, was raised by a she-wolf. I have come across many statues depicting a she-wolf suckling two young boys, which represents Romulus and Remus and the origins of Rome. Originally run by kings, the monarchy was abolished in 509 BC and replaced by the Roman Republic, elected officials, a senate and assemblies. The Roman Empire was founded in 27 BC. Infamous leaders included Julius Ceasar and Gaius Augustus.

Considering Roman achievements always takes me to the wonderful Monty Python sketch in one of my favourite films, *The Life of Brian* … 'What did the Romans ever do for us?'

Governance and Law: Roman law became the foundation for legal systems in many modern nations. The principle of 'innocent until proven guilty' and codifications like the Twelve Tables and later the Corpus Juris Civilis influenced legal traditions worldwide.

Engineering and Architecture: The Romans were master builders, creating durable roads, aqueducts, amphitheatres (the Colosseums in Rome and Verona) and monumental structures such as the Pantheon (Rome), the Aqueduct of Segovia (Spain), Pont Du Gard (France) and Hadrian's Wall (England). They pioneered the use of concrete, enabling large-scale construction.

Military Organisation: The Roman army, disciplined and innovative, was key to the empire's expansion. Its legions were supported by a sophisticated logistics system and advanced weaponry. At its height, the Roman Empire covered vast regions of Europe, North Africa and the Middle East, stretching across three continents. In the UK, the Roman Empire got as far as southern Scotland, and Hadrian's Wall was built to defend their empire from attacking Scottish tribes. They controlled 5 million square kilometres and a quarter of the world's population.

Culture and Religion: Roman culture was deeply influenced by the Greeks but also incorporated elements from other conquered peoples. Latin, the Roman language, became the basis for the Romance languages. The Romans also spread Christianity, which became the empire's official religion in the 4th century AD.

The Western Roman Empire declined because of a combination of internal and external factors, including economic difficulties, political corruption, military defeats and invasions, finally falling in 476 AD. The Eastern Roman Empire (Byzantine Empire) continued until the fall of Constantinople in 1453.

Middle Ages: 500–1400 AD

During the Middle Ages, Italy became a patchwork of city-states, duchies and papal territories. The Byzantine Empire controlled parts of the south, while the Papal States emerged as a powerful region in central Italy. The Italian city-states like Venice, Genoa, Florence and Milan flourished economically and culturally during the medieval period, benefitting from trade and their strategic positions in the Mediterranean.

This period was also marked by the rise of superpowers like England, France and the Holy Roman Empire and the devastation that was the Black Death, from 1347–1351, which killed a third of the population of Europe and up to 60% of the people of Italy.

Renaissance: 1400–1700 AD

Italy, specifically Florence, was the birthplace of the Renaissance, a cultural rebirth in art, science and philosophy. It marked a dramatic departure from the medieval world, or the Dark Ages, influenced by a renewed interest in classical art, culture and ideas of ancient Greece and Rome. The Renaissance had a profound impact not only on Italy but on all of Europe, shaping the development of Western civilisation. It was founded on the belief in humanism, i.e. the value of the individual experience and the potential of human beings, especially through education.

Florence during this period was an exceptionally wealthy region, and the likes of Cosimo de' Medici (1389–1464) followed by Lorenzo de' Medici (1449–1492) and Piero de' Medici (1472–1503) empowered and paid for much of the initial Renaissance, along with the Catholic

Church and the Sforza family in Milan. The Renaissance produced some of the most iconic and influential art in history. Renaissance artists sought to depict the human form realistically, using techniques like perspective to create depth and the illusion of space. They also focused on individual expression, naturalism and idealised human beauty.

It wasn't a rebirth only of art and architecture but also of scientific discovery and inquiry, taking a seismic shift away from previous religious explanations to the requirement for observations and experimentation. Galileo Galilei (1564–1642), often called the father of modern science, was instrumental in this work.

The following are important figures within this period, listed with their famous works. A mixture of sculptures, painters, politicians, philosophers, humanists, architects, historians, poets, writers and military leaders:

- Leonardo da Vinci (1452–1519) Mona Lisa, The Last Supper, Vitruvian Man
- Michelangelo Buonarroti (1475–1564) David, Pietà, Sistine Chapel ceiling
- Raphael (Raffaello Sanzio) (1483–1520) The School of Athens, The Sistine Madonna, Transfiguration
- Niccolò Machiavelli (1469–1527) The Prince, Discourses on Livy
- Francesco Petrarca (1304–1374) Canzoniere (Songbook), Secretum
- Giovanni Boccaccio (1313–1375) The Decameron
- Donatello (1386–1466) David, St. George, Equestrian Statue of Gattamelata
- Titian (Tiziano Vecellio) (c. 1488–1576) Venus of Urbino, Assumption of the Virgin, The Rape of Europa
- Giorgio Vasari (1511–1574) Lives of the Most Excellent Painters, Sculptors, and Architects

- Sandro Botticelli (1445–1510) The Birth of Venus, Primavera
- Andrea Palladio (1508–1580) Villa Rotonda, Basilica Palladiana
- Ludovico Ariosto (1474–1533) Orlando Furioso
- Leonardo Bruni (1370–1444) History of the Florentine People
- Cesare Borgia (1475–1507) military leader and political figure
- Michelangelo Merisi da Caravaggio (1571–1610) The Calling of Saint Matthew, Judith Beheading Holofernes

Napoleonic period: 1796–1815

Napoleon's influence and effect on Italy does have mixed reviews. He attacked Italy and the then-controlling Austrian Empire and placed himself as King of a unified Italy, concurrently when Emperor of France. He placed many of his family members in positions of power, which wasn't popular with Italians, as they saw this as a conquest rather than liberation. His popularity wasn't helped by the introduction of conscription, requiring Italian men to fight for the French Napoleonic cause.

However, Napoleon did spread the Napoleonic Code, a system of laws that emphasised equality before the law, property rights and civil liberties. These reforms modernised legal and administrative systems in many Italian states. He improved infrastructure, including the construction of roads and bridges, which helped facilitate trade and communication across Italy. He reformed the tax system, implemented modern banking practices and promoted industrial development in several regions. So, a mixed review. After the fall of Napoleon in 1815, the feeling of unification was strong within the Italians. The positive Napoleonic reforms, coupled with the French revolution, inspired many to seek a unified Italy.

Italian Unification (or the Risorgimento): 1861

Prior to the unification of 1861, and post-Napoleon, Italy returned to being divided into a number of disparate states: the Kingdom of Sardinia-Piedmont, the Kingdom of the Two Sicilies, the Kingdom of Naples, the Papates controlled by the Pope, and the Duchies of Parma, Modena, and Tuscany, as well as parts of Venetia and Lombardy that were controlled by Austria. The Italians use the term *Risorgimento* (meaning resurgence) for the Italian Unification. The journey towards unification was inspired by many revolutionary movements that were happening throughout Europe at that time. Uprisings happened in many Italian cities, the populace calling for reform and independence from foreign rule. Famously, in 1860, Garibaldi led his 1,000 Redshirts in a war against the Kingdom of the Two Sicilies and gained control of most of southern Italy – hugely significant in the movement toward unification. The Kingdom of Italy was decreed in 1861, with Victor Emmanuel II proclaimed monarch. March the 17th is celebrated as Unity Day (*Giornata dell'Unità Nazionale*).

20th Century

In 1915, during WW1, after initially declaring neutrality, Italy sided with the Allies on the understanding and agreement with the British, that, if the Allies won, Italy would regain disputed land from Austria-Hungary. The Italians fought an incredibly difficult and bloody campaign in the mountains in the north of Italy. Many of the Via Ferrata, near impossible man-made mountain routes, still exist today through the Alps, and are used by tourists as adrenalin walks. In 1922, Benito Mussolini and his Fascists rose to power making Italy a near-fascist dictatorship closely aligned with Hitler in Germany. They joined Germany during WW2 but switched sides in 1943 after Mussolini was dismissed first by the Fascist Committee and then by

King Victor Emmanuel III. Although Mussolini's reign is often defined as a fascist dictatorship, he was still under a certain degree of control by the Fascist Committee and Monarch. He was captured near Lake Como in Northern Italy when trying to flee to Switzerland in 1945, and was summarily executed by partisans and hung by the feet from a filling station roof in Milan.

The Germans were in Italy when the Italians switched sides. This area where I live was a hotbed of Italian resistance and the civilian population paid a heavy price for any attacks against the Germans. The Allies first landed in Italy during the Invasion of Sicily in July 1943, culminating in the German surrender and full liberation of Italy in May 1945. Post WW2, as early as 1946, Italy became a republic and abolished the monarchy.

Modern Italy

Italy has the third-largest economy in the EU and is a leader in luxury goods, car and food exports. However, it struggles with public debt, youth unemployment and regional economic problems. It rates top in cultural significance, historical impact, food, drink and tourism, but struggles mid-table with the economy, innovation and technology, education and research, and environmental efforts. Italy scores high on quality of life and life expectancy, healthcare, and lifestyle. Its Mediterranean climate, rich culture and slower pace of life are attractive and are what brought me here. It is a founding member of the EU and Nato, a member of the G7 and has a population of 60 million people.

Chapter 16
Puccini, *Carnevale* and Day-Tripping

As I write, this year marks the centenary of the passing of Giacomo Puccini (1858–1924), a master of opera whose works have captivated the hearts of many, including myself. To celebrate this monumental anniversary, the Teatro del Popolo in my local town hosted a splendid evening dedicated to his legacy. It was an event that wrapped the audience in a rich celebration of his compositions: *Tosca*, *Madame Butterfly*, *Turandot* and *La Bohème*.

The setting for the evening was the beautifully restored theatre, a gem tucked away in this quiet town, far from the hustle you might expect of such a cultural gathering. Dressed rather casually – I hadn't anticipated it to be a tuxedo affair – I soon realised I had missed the memo about the dress code. Undeterred, I made my way to the bar and confidently ordered a glass of Chianti in my newfound Italian. But rather than ask for a glass of wine, I had accidentally, and loudly, asked for a 'bicycle of wine'. When the barmaid looked puzzled, I again confidently requested a 'bicycle of Chianti' … Oh dear.

As the evening went on, the air filled with the powerful and poignant arias from Puccini's operas. Each note played by the orchestra and sung by the opera singers seemed to float around the room. It was truly enchanting, sending us all into a mesmerising trance. There's a peculiar magic to live opera, especially pieces as emotional and dramatic as those written by Puccini. Whether it was the desperate love of *Tosca* or the tragic beauty of *Madame Butterfly*, each aria was a reminder of Puccini's genius in capturing human emotions.

The performances were magnificent, each singer bringing a unique flavour and depth to the songs. Being in the presence of such artistry, witnessing the raw power of voice and music intertwined, was truly an experience that was beyond ordinary. It was a night where the present met the past, where the echoes of Puccini's life filled the space as intense as the music itself. Recalling the events of the evening, it wasn't just the magnificence of the theatre or the elegance of the crowd that made it memorable, but the sheer joy of being part of a community coming together to honour a legend. These memories, like the melodies of Puccini, linger long after the curtain falls. If you ask me, they remind us of the beauty and drama that life, at its best, mirrors the operas that I love so much – minus the murder, of course. It was a night that celebrated more than just music; it celebrated life itself in all its unexpected, chaotic and beautiful moments.

In Italy, Carnival (*Carnevale*) isn't just for larger cities such as Venice; it's a big deal everywhere, even in my small town. Here, everyone from babies in pushchairs to people over a hundred years old come together to celebrate the last day of Carnival. It's a fun day filled with laughter and fancy-dress costumes, as all the local school children get dressed up as pirates, fairies and all sorts of fun characters. Their faces are painted, and they all look amazing. You'll see grandparents sitting on benches, all wrapped up and smiling as they watch the children play. Mums and dads are busy too, trying to keep an eye on their little ones while chatting with friends and neighbours.

You will find stalls everywhere selling treats like hot churros and thick, warm hot chocolate, which absolutely everyone loves – including me. It's perfect for keeping warm and adds to the sweet smells filling the air. The music being pumped through the town is a mixture of old folk songs and catchy pop tunes, which keeps us dancing and adds to the atmosphere. It's the kind of day where no one worries about everyday stuff. As it gets later, nobody wants to stop. The children seem to have endless energy. There's laughter everywhere and groups of friends are showing off their dance moves in the town square, with everyone cheering them on.

San Vivaldo – Just ten minutes from my home is San Vivaldo. I stumbled across this Tuscan experience everyone should see if they are in this area – it's a hidden gem. What I found was a monastery, but not just any monastery. This place holds a unique piece of history that's both fascinating and a bit unexpected, especially for someone like me who isn't religious.

In the early 1500s, when the Ottoman Empire controlled Jerusalem, Christians couldn't visit the holy sites. To help the faithful feel connected to these sacred places, the Catholic Church did something quite extraordinary. They built what's now known as the 'Jerusalem of Tuscany' right here in Italy. It's a replica of Jerusalem, originally with 35 chapels, each one mirroring an important site from the holy city. They then encouraged those with a Catholic faith to make the pilgrimage to the holy sites, right here in Western Europe.

Walking through San Vivaldo is like stepping into a storybook of the past. Although only 18 of the original chapels remain, each one is a treasure trove of art and history. They were built to face the same direction as their counterparts in Jerusalem and were crafted with such care to detail. It's like a bridge across time and geography, created to bring Jerusalem to those who couldn't make the original pilgrimage.

When wandering through the chapels, I was struck by the beautiful terracotta sculptures telling the story of Christ's last couple of weeks. There was something incredibly moving about seeing those scenes depicted so vividly. One chapel in particular caught my eye. It housed the Last Supper, complete with the figures of Christ and his disciples and even Judas, holding the infamous bag of silver.

You might think a place like this would feel solemn, but when I was there, I felt the air around me to be peaceful in such a way that's hard to describe. It's quiet, yes, but it's a reflective kind of quiet that makes you think, even if you're not religious. It's amazing to think about how people centuries ago walked these grounds for solace and spiritual reflection, much like I was doing.

The craftsmanship of the chapels is something else. Each building and every sculpture tell part of a story, and, despite the years, the essence of what they represent remains intact. It's not just a walk through a religious site, but also a journey through art, history and faith all rolled into one. It's clear that San Vivaldo is something special, a slice of Jerusalem tucked away in Tuscany. Though I set out that day without expecting much, I left with a profound sense of having connected with something timeless. This 'Jerusalem of Tuscany' isn't just a site for those with religious fervour. It's a place that invites anyone with a curiosity for history, a passion for art, or simply a love for exploring the hidden corners of the world.

Siena – Another noteworthy day-trip I had was to Siena. It was a crisp January morning with blue skies as I boarded the train. I've always cherished these clear, sunny winter days. Arriving in Siena, I opted to walk from the train station to the historical city centre, a walk of only about 20 minutes. While there were options to take a bus or a taxi, walking seemed the best way to soak in the city's atmosphere and beauty. Walking through a location gives you a chance to see things you might otherwise miss.

The heart of Siena is absolutely stunning. I made my way down to the main square, known for hosting the Palio, a famous horse race that's an incredible spectacle, run twice a year during the summer. Imagine a bustling square packed with thousands of locals and visitors, from which people watch a horserace around the square, cheering passionately for their district's horse and rider. During the race the surrounding buildings are also decked out with scaffolding to provide the best views of the Palio. It was easy to imagine the excitement that would fill the air during the race, with the entire city coming alive in a vibrant celebration of local tradition and competition.

Not far from the square, I visited Siena Cathedral, or *Il Duomo*. Constructed between 1215 and 1296, the cathedral is a masterpiece of Gothic architecture. The detail on the front façade is particularly breathtaking, with intricate carvings that invite you to pause and appreciate the craftsmanship.

Siena is also a haven for food lovers. The city boasts numerous authentic osterias where you can indulge in traditional Tuscan cuisine. I was particularly charmed by a small pizza shop not far from the cathedral, where delicious slices of pizza were on offer for just a few euros. It's places like these that cater not just to tourists but also to locals and students, making great food accessible to everyone.

As I wandered through the city, every corner seemed to hold a new delight. From the bustling square to the serene beauty of the cathedral and the simple joy of a pizza slice savoured on a sunny step, Siena was a blend of historical grandeur and everyday pleasures. It's a city that truly captivated my heart, making for a memorable day filled with discovery and enjoyment.

Cinque Terre – I remember vividly the day I decided to visit Cinque Terre. It started at Pisa Central Station, where I hopped on a train, eager to explore this famed region. Cinque Terre, or Five Lands, comprises five quaint towns nestled along the Italian coast, and I was about to discover just how charming they could be. The train cuts straight through mountains, plunging into darkness before emerging into the daylight at each town – a thrilling experience. Despite a bit of a rocky start with a broken-down train and a missed connection that set me back a few hours, I finally arrived, three hours late but still excited.

Each town in Cinque Terre, – Monterosso, Vernazza, Corniglia, Manarola and Riomaggiore – boasts a unique charm, but they all share a common thread: a vibrant life connected deeply with the sea. The seafood, as you can imagine, was a highlight. Every restaurant seemed to boast its own boat, sitting on its doorstep.

Walking around Manarola, I was struck by the steepness of the valley sides and how every centimetre of land as far as you could see was cultivated. Grapes, lemons, limes and oranges grew in abundance, painting the landscape with bursts of green and vibrant citrus colours.

The next day, I visited Riomaggiore, just a two-minute train ride from where I stayed. It was larger than Manarola and had a reputation as a livelier spot, with more bars and a younger, more-energetic vibe. Despite visiting off-season on a quiet Sunday morning in January, I could sense the potential for fun and festivity. The town, while weathered, felt authentic and brimmed with life waiting to burst forth in the busier months. I imagined the streets buzzing with locals and tourists, and the air filled with music, laughter and the clinking of glasses. These towns are places of beauty, steeped in a rich history and colourful culture. For anyone thinking of visiting, I'd recommend coming in the warmer months to experience the lively atmosphere and stunning natural scenery. But be aware – they'll be packed.

Cinque Terre left a lasting impression on me. It's a place where the beauty of nature meets human creativity and resilience. The towns are built into the landscape in ways that seem almost unimaginable, with homes perched precariously, yet perfectly, on cliffs. The sense of community is palpable, with every local seeming to embrace life by the sea. If I were to return, I'd spend more time in Riomaggiore to soak up its lively atmosphere. But for those seeking quieter moments, Manarola would be the spot. Either way, Cinque Terre is a must-visit, a spot that deserves a place on any travel lover's bucket list. It's not just about the stunning views or the delicious food, but also about experiencing a way of life that celebrates both the challenges and joys of coastal living.

Vinci – Visiting Leonardo da Vinci's birthplace in Vinci was like stepping back in time, to a place where one of the greatest minds of the Renaissance first explored the world. Born to a notary father and a young peasant mother, Leonardo didn't have a surname or the privilege of a formal education because of his status as an illegitimate child. Yet this didn't hold him back; rather, it set the stage for a life of extraordinary self-taught achievements.

As a young lad, Leonardo roamed the forests around Vinci, sketching birds, animals and insects with a keen eye that captured every detail. His talent was nurtured by his supportive uncle and grandfather, who encouraged his interest in the arts. When he was just a teen, his life took a significant turn. His father, still involved in his life, introduced him to an artist in Florence who took Leonardo under his wing and helped hone his growing skills.

Leonardo wasn't just a painter; he was a master of many crafts. He delved deep into anatomy, attending over 30 dissections, which enabled him to draw the human body with astounding accuracy. His sketches of muscles, ligaments, intestines and brains were so precise that they almost mirrored reality.

His inventive mind didn't stop at art. Leonardo created the concepts for the first tank, parachute, and he even sketched designs for an aeroplane and a helicopter, centuries before such machines were actually built. Over 200 drawings of his inventions lie in his notebooks that went unrecognised for 400 years. If his ideas had been discovered earlier, the course of technological history would have been vastly different. Despite his genius in invention, including military devices, Leonardo was a man of profound compassion. He was a vegetarian, believing strongly that animals felt pain. He would often buy caged birds at the market just to set them free. This contrast in his character, between the creator of war machines and the gentle liberator of birds, paints a picture of a deeply thoughtful individual wrestling with the complexities of life.

The highlight of my visit was seeing the house where he spent the first 12 years of his life. Now transformed into a museum, it houses a cinema room where Leonardo appears as a hologram, bringing the artist and inventor to life in a way that feels both surreal and intimate. Another fascinating discovery was his use of mirror script. Leonardo wrote from right to left, a technique that kept his left hand from smudging his work, which was only readable with the aid of a mirror.

It's clear that Leonardo da Vinci was more than just a figure from a history book. He was a visionary whose ideas transcended the limitations of his time and a person whose humanity coloured his scientific and artistic endeavours.

San Gimignano – a place steeped in history and brimming with charm. As I walked through the ancient streets, I was struck by the beauty and significance of this historic borgo. Behind me stood the grand entrance gate, welcoming me into a world that seemed frozen in time. San Gimignano – often referred to as the Medieval Manhattan or the Town of Fine Towers – is a gem in the heart of Tuscany. This nickname comes from the skyline of medieval towers that once dominated the landscape. These towers were more than just architectural feats; they were symbols of power and wealth. As I wandered through the town, the history and stories behind these towering structures came alive.

The town's origins date back to the Etruscan period, but it was during the medieval era that San Gimignano truly flourished. By the 12th and 13th centuries, the town had become an important centre of trade and finance. Wealthy families built towers to display their prosperity and influence, leading to a fierce competition that saw the skyline filled with over 70 towers at its peak. It was said that the taller the tower, the more powerful the family.

Standing in the main square, Piazza della Cisterna, I couldn't help but marvel at the remaining towers. Only 14 have survived the passage of time, yet they still convey the grandeur of the town's heyday. The square itself is named after the central well that provided water to the town's inhabitants. Surrounded by medieval houses, shops and cafés, it was easy to imagine the bustling life of centuries past.

One of the highlights of my visit was indulging in the local *gelato* (ice cream). San Gimignano is famous for its *gelaterie* (gelaterias), and two of the best can be found right in the heart of the town. I couldn't resist trying a scoop (or two) of the award-winning gelato. The rich, creamy flavours were a delight, perfectly complementing the warm Tuscan sun. From Piazza della Cisterna, I moved to the second main square, Piazza del Duomo. Here, the Collegiate Church of San Gimignano, with its stunning frescoes depicting scenes from the Old and New Testaments, offers a glimpse into the artistic legacy of the town. These frescoes were painted by some of the most renowned artists of the time, including Domenico Ghirlandaio and Benozzo Gozzoli.

When there, I learned about the fascinating history of the towers.

The competition to build the tallest tower became so intense that it led to disputes and acrimony among the town's leading families. To bring some order to the chaos, the local council decided to build a communal tower, known as *la Torre Grossa* (the big tower), and declared that no other tower could be taller. This decision helped to curb the rivalry and maintain a semblance of peace in the town. As I continued my exploration, I couldn't help but reflect on the significance of these towers. They were more than just symbols of wealth; they were part of the town's identity, representing the ambition and drive of its people. The towers stood as silent witnesses to the ebb and flow of history, revealing the resilience and ingenuity of those who built them.

San Gimignano's charm extends beyond its architecture and history. The town is also known for its exquisite wine, Vernaccia di San Gimignano. This white wine, made from the Vernaccia grape, has been produced in the region since the Renaissance. I couldn't leave without sampling some of this local treasure. Sitting in a quaint café, sipping Vernaccia and soaking in the view of the medieval towers was an experience to cherish. The town's rich history is complemented by its vibrant culture. Throughout the year, San Gimignano hosts various festivals and events that celebrate its heritage. One such event is the *Ferie delle Messi* (harvest festival), a medieval festival, held in June, that brings the town's history to life with parades, music and traditional games. Visiting during such a festival offers a unique opportunity to see San Gimignano in all its historical splendour.

Chapter 17
Paying It Forward and 20 Years Left

This book is slightly more than just my first year in Tuscany, I've also added in a couple of experiences I'd like to share. Some of you might not know, but the legendary Concorde – that supersonic marvel of aviation – once graced Belfast back in August 1987. I was just 17 at the time brimming with the recklessness and adventure that comes with youth. I was supposed to be flying British Airways from Belfast International to London Heathrow, a journey ordinary in every sense, except it turned out to be anything but. It was the event that made me look beyond myself and caused me to experience an epiphany – something I still try to do to this very day. Back then, my life was in a state of exciting flux. I had left home and was living on my own, absorbing the exhilarating and daunting experiences of early adulthood.

During a couple of weeks off from my job, I had returned home to Northern Ireland to visit my family and friends, before flying back to England. When I arrived at Aldergrove (now Belfast International), to return to England, the atmosphere was electric, buzzing with an unexpected fervour that piqued my curiosity immediately. I was clueless about the cause until I reached the check-in area. Back in those days, the options were fairly straightforward: no Ryanair, no EasyJet, just British Airways, British Midland or walking/swimming. I approached the BA desk, baggage in tow, to check in for my scheduled 10.30 am flight. As I did, I couldn't help but ask, 'What's all this commotion about?' The lady behind the desk informed me there was an airshow happening that very day, and that Concorde was the star of the show. If you still search for the image of the aeroplane, you will get to see what a magnificent marvel of aviation it was.

My heart skipped a beat. The thought of seeing Concorde was thrilling. Air travel regulations weren't as stringent back then, so I cheekily inquired if I could switch to the last flight out, allowing me some time to enjoy the airshow: 'Absolutely, Concorde's here today, and it's heading back at half-four.' That was all the encouragement I needed. I asked, half-jokingly, half-hopeful, if there was any chance I could snag a seat on Concorde for the return leg. 'No, no, absolutely not,' she laughed, 'though there might be a couple of seats left, you never know.' That glimmer of possibility was enough for me. I decided to linger and explore the possibilities.

So, there I was, standing at my check-in desk from half past nine in the morning, apparently for a half-ten flight, but really, I was now part of the airshow crowd. I watched jets slicing through the sky, acrobatic and graceful, each loop and swoop raising the stakes of my excitement. Time passed in a surreal blend of airshow antics and the ordinary rituals of travel, bathroom breaks, grabbing a burger, returning to my vantage point to gaze up at another jet thundering overhead. All in all, it was a good show and a memorable experience, but the climax was yet to come.

As the hours slipped by, my position in the check-in queue slipped. From first, I found myself sixth, then seventh, and by mid-afternoon, about tenth. The queue was alive with chatter and speculation about Concorde. And then, in a flourish, the British Airways desk hoisted a silver board displaying the tickets for Concorde. There weren't many – if I remember correctly, about sixty. That set my heart racing. For all I knew, all my waiting and the time spent in the hope of riding the legendary Concorde would not be in vain.

But … first, the journalists and VIPs descended, plucking tickets with hurried entitlement, followed by other dignitaries. The stack of tickets dwindled dramatically, from sixty to fifty to twenty-five, down to twenty. My heart sank each time the number was reduced. The announcements began urging us to abandon hope for Concorde and take the shuttle flight instead. 'Don't wait for Concorde; it's not going to happen for you,' they said. But something in me resisted. I decided to wait it out, clinging to the fading hope of securing a spot. Now, I cannot say for sure what it was that prompted me to hold on so tightly to the hope that I, too, would be flying in Concorde, but whatever it was – divine intervention, gut instinct, hope, or me pushing my luck – was about to be put to the test that would be nerve-wracking for me, albeit even for a fraction of time.

By the time Concorde landed and completed its part in the show, the tickets had reduced to a precious few. I was now 13th in the queue, clinging desperately to the hope of being one of the last to board. The final distribution of tickets began, and it was as nail-biting as any suspense thriller. The operations manager, with a solemnity befitting the occasion, started handing out the last tickets. For the first time, my heart started to let go of the hope I had been clinging on to so tightly a mere moment ago as the remaining tickets started to disappear. Finally, the distribution came down to me and another chap. We were the last two hopefuls, the final barrier between aspiration and reality. The gentleman before me received the last ticket … ticket 12 … none left. I'd missed out by one seat.

I'll never forget what happened next. The man turned to me, his face a mixture of sympathy and respect, and said, 'You've been here since half nine this morning, haven't you? Take it. You deserve this more.' And just like that, he handed me the last ticket – the golden ticket, if you will. How could he have done that? I mean the sheer generosity, though it may not seem like much to you as you read this. If only I had the words to describe it appropriately. The joy and disbelief melded into a surge of gratitude. I snatched the ticket, mumbling my thanks, too overwhelmed to formulate proper gratitude.

Boarding Concorde was surreal. As I settled into my seat, the smallest window beside me offered a view of the world I was about to see in a way I never had before. We took off, joined briefly in formation by the Red Arrows over the Isle of Man, putting on a display that matched the extraordinary nature of our flight. This was going to be the ride of a lifetime, and I was but a lucky youngster to take a gamble, and it had paid off only because of the generosity of a kind soul.

The captain, sensing the excitement bubbling over in the cabin, offered us one more surprise. 'Who wants to go supersonic?' he asked. Of course, the answer was a unanimous and enthusiastic yes. He turned Concorde right, out towards the Atlantic and accelerated to supersonic, the screens in front of us showing our incredible speed.

That day, that flight changed something in me. It wasn't just about the thrill of supersonic travel or the luxury of smoked salmon, champagne and Concorde socks. It was about the kindness of strangers, the serendipity of moments that define us. I was given a gift by a man with a golden heart, and ever since I've tried to pass on that kindness to keep the spirit of that extraordinary day alive in every interaction.

Perhaps the purpose of recounting this precious memory and making it a part of my book is to share with you the kindness I got to witness and experience from a complete stranger that drastically impacted the way I perceive things. The sheer act of selflessness and putting others before yourself can be more rewarding than we give it credit for. If it were up to me, I would make it mandatory for everyone to experience such generosity often so that the flames of paying it forward would burn bright in our hearts and minds. It is not something that can be taught. It is something that comes from within. Something that makes you want to surrender yourself in front of another. And no, it is not a real sacrifice, and for you, it may not even matter much. But for some young bloke out there, it might be a life-altering experience that would prompt them to adapt to the mindset of showing the same act of kindness and gratitude to others.

I've learned lessons throughout my life and the following is another such story from the early 1980s involving a family member who worked in the Metropolitan Police in London. During that time, George Best, a football legend considered by many to be among the greatest players of all time, found himself on a downward spiral. His glory days on the pitch were behind him, replaced by his struggles with alcohol. One day, he was arrested for drink driving in central London, a low point for a man who had once been at the pinnacle of his sport. Brought into the station where my relative was stationed, George Best became the centre of attention, not for his achievements, but for his fall from grace. Senior officers, drawn by the celebrity, came to look at him, yet offered no warmth or hospitality. In fact, one explicitly ordered my relative not to extend the simple courtesy of making Best a cup of tea or coffee.

Despite the direct order, my relative chose compassion over compliance, walked to a coffee shop next to the station and bought him a large coffee and some doughnuts. She didn't make Best a coffee as ordered; she bought him one. Although he was in no condition to fully express his gratitude, the gesture itself spoke volumes. This act of kindness, small yet defiant, has been a guiding example in my life. It taught me the importance of following one's heart, of recognising when to sidestep regulations in favour of human decency.

We live in a world bound by countless rules, regulations and expectations. Yet, what my relative demonstrated through her actions was the power of individual choice and kindness. She showed that, even in the face of authority, one can choose to act with compassion. Her decision to care for someone in need, despite being told otherwise, underscores a fundamental truth: doing the right thing often means listening to your heart.

Like I said, this book is more than just about me moving to Italy. It is about sharing a small number of good experiences that have shaped me. I try and recall all the good times I have had with my family, my parents, siblings, children, and all the new and exciting memories I am making in Italy. Perhaps these are the best ones in my memory catalogue, which explains my enthusiasm to share them with you.

Growing up, I watched my grandparents and my parents age gracefully within the familiar confines of their lives. They never had the inclination, nor the opportunity, to venture far from home. It simply never crossed their minds. Meanwhile, there I was in the north coast of Northern Ireland, 53 years old, gazing out of my window as a new empty-nester, feeling a growing restlessness stirring within me. I didn't just want a change; I was craving it. I longed for the warmth of the sun, for new challenges, to remain engaged with life and continue being an interested and interesting person.

Reaching out through social media, I know I'm not alone. Many of you have share similar sentiments about wanting more from life as we age. The following is what I believe: at 53, I have 20 years left of vitality, optimism and strength. By the time you hit your early to mid-70s, you might not want to embark on life-altering journeys, might not yearn for new experiences, or possess the same zest for outgoing adventures as I do now, in the prime of my early fifties. There are always exceptions – and superb if you know someone in their 80s who is still full of life. For me, the realisation was clear – if there was ever a time to act, it was now.

Life gives us about 70 years, if we're lucky, to really make something of our time here. I didn't want my days in my mid-fifties filled watching the rain beat against the windows, wondering what might have been, huddling up to a fire and closing the curtains against wild and windy days. I wanted my days to be vibrant and full of purpose. I wanted to wake up each morning with the possibility of something new: 'Today, I'll wander through a bustling market', 'Today, I'll visit a local festival', 'Today, I'll swim 50 lengths in my pool', 'Today, I'll challenge myself to learn ten more words in Italian'. This was the thought process that guided my decision to move to Italy. It was about seizing the opportunity. It was about transforming the 'possibly' into the 'absolutely'. It was a decision to actively choose life in a place that promised sunshine and the opportunity to continuously learn and grow, not just exist. I wanted adventure.

Do I have any regrets? Not yet. Every morning, when I open my curtains – not to gauge the heaviness of the rain, but to greet the day

– I'm reminded why I made this choice. The decision to move was not just about changing my surroundings but about enhancing my quality of life. It was about ensuring that my years were not just about reminiscence, but about being present in the joy of the moment, about making every day interesting and fulfilling.

So, for those wondering 'Why Italy? Why move?', it's simple. It was time to shift from grey skies to active participation in a sun-filled life. Italy offered me a canvas to paint my days with vibrant colours of engagement and learning, a place where every day could be as mundane or as magical as I chose to make it. It's about living fully, not just living through. Don't wait for perfect conditions – create them. Don't settle for watching life from the sidelines – dive into it. Make your life a series of deliberate choices. That's the beauty of being at this stage of life: we have the wisdom to appreciate what matters most and the energy to act on it. It won't be for everyone, but it was right for me. Will I stay here forever? I simply don't know, but I hope I can inspire others who are in the position to do so, to go for it – but only after you have done your research.

Chapter 18
Tuscan Coastline and Outdoor Living

Although I'm nestled within the heart of the Tuscan countryside, it does have a coastline, about an hour away to the west from me. A lot of the locals disappear to the coast in August to holiday, generations usually sharing one household for a month.

I'm out and about today along the coast, and I've just stopped in front of the Castello Mediceo di Livorno, which commands the view, a formidable structure dating back to the 16th century. Built by the Medici as a bulwark against pirates, it was transformed in the 19th century into a grand single residence and, later, into apartments. It's a striking feature of the coastline, a reminder of the lengths to which the Medici went to protect this stretch of Italy. Along the coast, similar fortifications tell of old threats and the perpetual guard against them, their historic presence adding to the beauty of the coastline.

Moving further down the coast, you will arrive in Castiglioncello. This place captures the essence of the Italian seaside with perfection. Here, the boats in the harbour are nothing short of stunning, gleaming under the sun, their sleek forms speaking of wealth and leisure. While their price tags might deter a mere observer like me, their beauty is free to admire, and I did so.

Imagine yourself sitting by the sea in Castiglioncello, a canvas of vibrant greens and deep blues stretching out before you. The sunlight dances on the water, creating a sparkle that seems magical. As you bask in the warmth of the sun, a profound peace settles around you. From Pisa down to Livorno and further along the coast towards Rome, the Tyrrhenian Sea, part of the vast Mediterranean, is a constant companion, its gentle waves a soothing presence.

The coastal Tuscan life is vividly Mediterranean. Artists set up their easels by the shore, capturing the ever-changing play of light on water. Markets buzz with the day's catch and the vibrant chatter of traders. Children dash in and out of the water, their laughter a bright note against the steady rhythm of the waves. As evening draws in, the seaside eateries come alive. The setting sun casts long shadows and bathes everything in a golden hue, enhancing the flavours of local dishes being savoured by diners. The air is thick with the aroma of seafood and wine, and conversations meander like the gentle tide.

In Castiglioncello, each day closes as it begins, with the sea whispering to those who walk its shores. It's a place that holds the past in its architecture and the present in its lively marina, a perfect blend that captures the essence of Tuscan coastal life. I can say that here I discovered a rhythm that resonates with the beat of the sea and the warmth of the sun, a serene accompaniment to the days spent in one of the most picturesque parts of Italy. That's yet another thing that I absolutely love about this country. There are adventures and marvellous sights to see no matter where you go. They say home is where the heart is, and, if that's true, I am right at home and trying my darndest to make it work.

Gardening has always been one of my hobbies, but I cannot say I have pursued it with any vigour. I do love greenery, lush green gardens and beautiful flowers showcasing their colours. So, one morning I found myself wandering the aisles of a local garden centre, a newfound resolve in my step to add to my life here – in a sense, to add value to my life. It was here, among the lush greenery and the fragrant blooms, that a realisation dawned on me, not just about the move to this sun-drenched Tuscan town, but about the way I live now. My terrace, which I've come to see as a mirror to my apartment in both size and potential, had lain bare, unadorned since my arrival. In this land where life spills effortlessly outdoors, my terrace had been waiting, a canvas untouched.

When awake, I spend 95% of my time outdoors. It never occurred to me that my terrace is basically an abandoned garden waiting to be groomed and that I would spend so much time on it. Living here, you quickly learn that the boundary between indoors and outdoors blurs, the open air becomes your living room, the terrace a continuation of your space. It struck me that my terrace was as big as my apartment itself, yet it had remained an overlooked half of my living quarters. This realisation sparked a desire to transform it into a space as lived-in and loved as the interior. Beyond my terrace, I am surrounded by gardens and greenery, but that is taken care of by the condominium agency. The terrace is all mine, and I'm going to get stuck in.

The garden centre trip was more than a casual shopping outing. It was a mission. I was there to equip myself for a grand project – to bring life, colour and energy to my outdoor living space. My cart gradually filled with pots of jasmine (*gelsomino*) climbers, whose sweet scent would soon rise through the air. These climbers, I decided, would trace their way up the steps leading to my apartment, a fragrant welcome home.

In addition to the jasmine, I chose a variety of clematis for the pergola, envisioning a mass of blooms that would create a natural cascade of colour and texture. The vision of my terrace transforming into a blooming garden was motivating. It was about beautifying a space, certainly, but also about crafting an environment that reflected the life I wanted to lead here – outdoors, surrounded by nature, under a brilliant blue sky.

As I stood amidst the colours of the garden centre, the array of plants and flowers seemed infinite, each one a potential addition to my terrace garden. I selected herbs too – basil, thyme, rosemary – not just for their culinary uses but for their aromatic presence. These would sit along the edges of the terrace, their fragrances mingling with that of the jasmine and clematis.

Back home, the work began. Cleaning the terrace was the first step, scrubbing the stone to rid it of dust and grime – the lichen being particularly troublesome – preparing it as a fitting backdrop for the colour it was about to support. Next came the acid wash, a thorough treatment to ensure the brickwork was pristine, a clean slate on which to build my garden oasis.

The painting followed, refreshing the walls with colours chosen to complement the terracotta pots and the vibrant greens and purples of the plants. Each brushstroke felt like a declaration of intent, each colour a step closer to realising my vision of an outdoor living room. With the preparation complete, planting began. The physical act of embedding the plants in their new home was therapeutic, each root's placement a further entrenchment of my own roots in this new life. As the jasmine began its ascent up the steps, I imagined the future, how the climbers would eventually sprawl, creating a verdant curtain, a living entryway to my home.

This transformation of the terrace into a thriving garden is symbolic of my broader adaptation to life here. In Tuscany, where the sun sets late and the evenings stretch long, outdoor spaces become sanctuaries. My terrace, once a forgotten appendage of my living space, is now poised to become its heart. I have planned that in the days to come I'll continue this project, knowing that with each plant added, each arrangement attempted, I'm not just decorating a space but defining my home.

Now, three months on, and my terrace, with its blooms and scents, has been transformed, and it has become a brand-new space. One caveat, however: someone lets their herd of goats loose every winter to roam the hillsides. Last year, in the winter of 2023, when I had planted very little, twenty goats appeared on my terrace and devoured everything. They left no plant/greenery untouched. I can only hope that was a one-off.

The north coast of Northern Ireland was my home for many years, but for as long as I can remember my heart has always desired to be somewhere sunny, with clear blue skies and vast landscapes – a haven where serenity reigned. That was the kind of place my heart was demanding, and, by relocating to Italy, I have found that place. If this has struck a chord with you, then what you need to do is set out and find a place of similar potential for you. It's not for everyone. The majority of you will absolutely love where you live, and the weather will play a very minor role in your lives. Not for me – it controlled my inner self. I need the sun to lift my spirits and reveal my true, positive, optimistic self.

Living near family, living close to your children and friends, all of this is good. My children had moved to England and Scotland, and I was left in Northern Ireland under the same dark skies. I was presented with two options: either I could take the opportunity to truly spread my wings or I could go on with the life I had, the repetitive routine, the same skies, regular rainfall, and catching up with the same few people. For some, the latter is perfect – and I applaud that – but that wasn't for me.

Will I stay here forever? I'm not sure, but that's the beauty of it; my feet aren't cast in concrete. And if I decide to move closer to grandchildren in ten years' time, then that is what I will do. Now, though, I want a sun-blessed challenge, and that's what I've taken on. It has been a challenge, yes, but I am adamant about making it happen. Family is always important and an irreplaceable part of life. I see some of my Irish friends out here more often than I did in Ireland. I'd like to think it was me, but I know it's down to the swimming pool, sun and fine wine. I believe it's important to make friends from diverse backgrounds. Having friends around the globe is an achievement in my book, and I have made many, especially here in Tuscany.

No dream is too big or too little. But remember, every dream fulfilled is made of sheer will and dedication. The people you see making their dreams work are the ones who have made some gutsy moves and sacrificed many things, the most important of which is their comfort zone. They tore down walls and stepped outside, only to stare blankly into the eye of a dream and stand their ground in the face of uncertainty – and you will face a lot of it if you have truly decided to give in to your dreams. But the best thing about it is that uncertainty keeps things interesting.

Before deciding to move to Italy I had always wanted a career where I could take the entire month of January off and disappear to the sun. January in the UK and Ireland is a long, poor, depressing month, and I have always wanted to escape it. I wanted to spend January in a bright, sunny place, feeling the warmth of the sun on my face. It was here that I finally saw my wish become a reality when, in January 2024, I drove one morning, with my car window down, as the sun shone on my face. A pleasant 20 degrees made the sunlight all the more enjoyable, mending the pain of seasonal darkness that I had felt for such a significant period of my life. I cannot put into words the feeling – the ecstatic joy and happiness of seeing a big bright sun in the month of January. It just utterly melted all my troubles away and my spirits were at an all-time high. I'm not naïve enough to think that it is like this all the time. Tuscany is green for a reason, and we do get periods of heavy rain, but to see clear blue skies, 20 degrees and bright sunshine in January was food for my soul.

Your special place will do the same for you. It doesn't necessarily have to be the sun, but the sun does it for me. Your place could be a place of snow, it could be rainfall, it could be greenery, forests, gardens, or anything for that matter. If you do not find peace and happiness where you are, then make a move – research, make plans, organise and take solid concrete steps. You may possibly upset a few people close to you who won't understand your decision, but if you explain your reasoning they will come around and wish you well. Remember, you are doing this for yourself, not for anyone else. So, if it's for you, go for it, be determined. But remember it is not easy – it's not always sunshine, candyfloss and unicorns. You will come across many a dark moment and a questioning inner voice, but if you truly believe that this move is for you, keep at it and do not lose sight of your dreams. Let your passion be your guide.

Chapter 19
Searching for Yourself and Oenology

Now, I like a wee adventure. I'm a traveller and enjoy discovering new places and immersing myself in the scenic and artistic beauty of wherever I am. I'm someone who struggles forming real bonds and real connections with people. I'm just not a big fan. Although I do love to meet new people, interact with them, get to know them at surface level and share a tale or two, I am selectively extrovert. Being here has forced me to put a mirror to my true self. Oh dear, initially a painful experience.

The Italian culture has had a profound effect on me. The culture here is more community and family orientated, and they appear to live their lives outside of their homes, in the sun. This has made me reflect on where I have been and where I am now. This introspection starts with what I am grateful for. If I look back at my life, I have nothing but things to be happy and grateful about. My parents for having raised me this way, my siblings, my community surroundings, Portrush, the sea, my friends as a child, my friends as an adult, the Irish humour and all the people who had any kind of impact in shaping my personality. I'd like to be a stone lighter, yes, but aside from that, I am quite happy with how I turned out. I am proud of the confidence I have and the initiative I took to change my status from an empty-nester to a free spirit roaming Italy.

Though I have travelled to many places across the globe, I have not encountered any place as captivating, as invigorating, or as vibrant as Italy. My little home is far less grand than what I used to own, but, in my opinion, it is far more than anything I have ever had. I do miss my children, but thanks to technology, we are never further than a video call away.

The real question is – bear with me – how close are we to our true selves? Many of us never come across the realisation that, in the midst of the everyday grind, the only person we are getting more and more distant from is ourself. You may never come to realise this unless you take a walk alone, all by yourself, and then eventually, you peek out from underneath all of it and say hello.

I have had the opportunity to tread many long routes in solitude, miles upon miles of empty paths where I had no one but myself as a companion. Truthfully, initially I didn't have a clue who I was, as I was still to discover the true me. When the discover happened, I was delighted and mightily relieved. You find the real you in your reaction to solitude, events and people. Not everyone will want to find themselves. Not everyone will be the slightest bit interested in looking. If you are interested, it's about practising introspection. We are our own best friends. And be warned, this solitude that you spend with yourself can be (i) hard to get used to and then (ii) addictive.

Despite being a confident person, I have often found myself stranded and lost in an ocean of people. Having hordes of people around you is something that can be suffocating. I have been there, which is why I am able to recollect these experiences. The point is, don't lose yourself in the fast lane because the world will not stop. It is we who have to pause, stop, think and lend ourselves a helping hand. Rescue yourself and the process will be nothing short of an intellectual pilgrimage that you have taken – an endeavour that will help you reconnect with yourself and change your perspective on life. It will change how you see the world, the people, and how you carry yourself.

In my opinion, the best way to reveal yourself is to travel. Take baby steps, small, short trips. Explore. You never know what you will encounter on your way. The world is a big place. However, always exercise caution. Technology has made it easier, so just be prepared and have a backup plan – or, as I used to ensure my children had, an emergency fiver.

Here, in the heart of the Chianti country, I know someone who is an oenologist. He dedicates his life to the art and science of winemaking. His passion for crafting the perfect bottle of wine is testament to his dedication and love for this ancient practice. However, recent years have brought unforeseen challenges that even the most skilled winemakers could not have anticipated. Climate change has begun to leave its mark on this tranquil region, disrupting the delicate balance needed to produce exceptional wines. My friend Alessandro explained to me the complexities of these changes with a mix of scientific insight and concern.

'Drought,' he started, 'is one of our most pressing issues.' The lack of consistent water not only stresses the vines but also threatens the very survival of the vineyards. But water scarcity is not the only challenge. 'The rising temperatures are troubling,' he continued. Vines follow a rhythmic cycle through the seasons. Traditionally, they enter a period of dormancy during the colder months of December, January and February – a restorative sleep that allows them to conserve energy for the burst of growth in the spring.

However, this natural hibernation has been disrupted. The warmer winter temperatures have confused the vines, causing them to skip this crucial rest period. 'The vines haven't been going into hibernation as they should,' he lamented. This disruption not only affects the current season's growth but has long-term implications for the health of the vines and the quality of the grapes – the very foundation of wine production. For years now, this pattern has repeated, each warm winter further altering the landscape of winemaking. 'It's a problem we've been observing for several years,' he noted, with obvious concern in his voice.

In response to these challenges, my friend and his colleagues have been proactive. They're not just passive observers of these changes; they're at the forefront of seeking solutions. They experiment with new techniques and technologies, from adjusting irrigation practices to exploring different vine varieties more suited to changing climates. Their goal is not just to adapt but to preserve the integrity and legacy of their wines.

As we walked through the vineyards, the sun setting behind the hills, casting long shadows over the vines, he shared a piece of wisdom that has guided him through these trying times. 'Wine is more than a beverage. It's a narrative of the land, the climate and the people who cultivate it. Each bottle tells a story of its year, its struggles and its triumphs.' This perspective is what drives him and his peers to confront these challenges head-on. They understand that the essence of winemaking is found not just in the science of it, but in the harmony between nature and human endeavour. As the climate continues to change, they must evolve in order to find new ways to sustain this balance and ensure that the stories encapsulated in each bottle continue to be told.

Reflecting on his words, I realised that his struggle is a microcosm of a much larger battle. Across the globe, industries, communities and individuals are grappling with the effects of climate change. The lesson here, in the vineyards, is that adaptation and resilience are our most valuable tools. As we face these environmental challenges, there is wisdom in looking for guidance from those who work the land. Their intimate connection with nature, combined with scientific understanding, can lead the way in adapting to our changing world. Just as the winemaker adjusts his practices to protect his vines, so too must we all learn to safeguard our environment.

Later, as we sipped a glass of wine, there was a shared understanding that this bottle was more than the sum of its parts. It was a recognition of resilience, a beacon of hope that with passion, understanding and innovation, we can face the challenges ahead. And perhaps, in this shared experience, we find the true spirit of what it means to adapt and thrive in an ever-changing world.

In rural Tuscany, where the ancient and the modern blend seamlessly into the landscape, the people hold beliefs that are deeply rooted in the soil they work and in the faith they practise. Despite being in a country known for its strong religious convictions, the locals exhibit a level of superstition that often seems at odds with the orthodox doctrines of the church.

In many parts of the world, including the UK and Ireland, superstitions have evolved in alignment with popular myths and urban legends – such as the fear of Friday the 13th. Here in Tuscany, the people harbour their own distinct set of beliefs. In this part of Italy, it is not the 13th but rather the 17th that harbours ominous undertones. This peculiar dread is not arbitrary but is steeped in historical and cultural nuance that can be traced back to ancient Rome.

The fear of the 17th in Tuscany is intricately linked to the way Romans perceived the number. When written in Roman numerals, 17 is represented as XVII. This sequence, when rearranged, forms the word 'VIXI', which in Latin translates to 'I have lived' – a phrase inscribed on tombstones and perceived as a symbol of death. This linguistic twist turned the number 17 into a harbinger of bad luck and mortality, a stark reminder of life's fragility and the ever-present shadow of the afterlife.

This Tuscan superstition highlights how societies interpret and internalise the mysteries of life and death in different ways, each adding their own colours to human belief systems. The Tuscans, much like their ancient Roman ancestors, were reminded through these superstitions to live fully, to cherish each moment and to respect the forces, both seen and unseen, that governed their existence. It shows how different communities grappled with the unknown, each adding their voice to the chorus of human experience that sought to make sense of the world's mysteries.

Above: My escape spa close to my apartment.

Top right: My pool – I try to get in every day.

Below: Beautiful, elegant Italian Cypress trees.

Bottom right: Typical Tuscan first course (antipasti).

Above left: Pisa Tower.

Above: Teatro del Silenzio.

Below left: The Mercato Centrale, Florence.

Below: Replica of Michelangelo's David.

Above left and below: Florence.

Above: My favourite Tuscan city, Siena.

Below: Sunflower fields surround my town in the summer.

Above: A Giant of Peccioli.

Above right: Tinkerbell (my scooter).

Below: The 5.5 metre tall, 133-year-old Portrush Railway Station Clock.

Below right: Albert (my car).

Chapter 20
Getting Here Admin

I'm a mini adventurer by nature. The mundane life is not for me. I'm not talking about trying to find and navigate the Northwest Passage or walking solo to the South Pole. I'm talking about stepping outside your comfort zone boundaries. That in itself is an adventure. For some, moving abroad may be a possibility, but for others, it may not, given their responsibilities.

I am an empty-nester, as my children have left the nest. Before moving to Italy in 2023, I was all alone and, although I had a life outside my house, I had no responsibilities attached that would tie me to my hometown, which gave me a degree of freedom. Not everyone is that fortunate.

What you need to do is perform a comparative analysis of whether it is possible for you or not. What are your home responsibilities? How about financial liabilities? Do you have a plan for when you move? Income post move? Language barriers? The majority of people wanting to emigrate don't have a detailed plan, just a desire/passion to move abroad and start a new life. Unfortunately, desires and passion are only two of the vital ingredients for a successful move. Family ties, pounds/euros are as important as desire. For me it was a strategic, practical and calculated move that I had planned. It came a few years earlier than I had anticipated, but I hadn't appreciated how much being an empty-nester would affect me.

If you want to move abroad, do not be impulsive about it. Assess your situation logically. Think about your needs and wants, your desires, your income and your family. These are only some of the many factors you have to consider. Even though I have an Irish/EU passport, there were a number of issues that took me by surprise when I arrived – for example, you can't buy a car in Italy until you are an Italian resident, and that process in itself has numerous hurdles.

If you're considering moving abroad, the first thing you should do is research your destination. Wherever you are thinking of emigrating to is likely to be drastically different from where you have lived your whole life, so you need to invest some serious effort into learning about the place, the local customs, traditions and social norms. It will also be a very different place from the location you enjoy two weeks as a tourist every year, and the off-seasons can be harsh in terms of weather.

I made the mistake of not appreciating the volume and complexity of Italian bureaucracy. You could be struggling with multiple things, and, for all you know, the place and the people may not be compatible with you, and vice versa. So, if you want to integrate more seamlessly, you need to do your homework first.

Before you decide to move anywhere, you must consider the language. Research how different their language is from your primary language. Will your primary language help you stay afloat there? If not, you will have to take some language classes. Learn the language like your life depends on it. You can use apps such as Duolingo, but doing so lacks the immersion factor. As an English language teacher, I know for a fact that many of my students are becoming more and more proficient in speaking English (albeit with an Irish accent) because I am asking that they speak only English in my classroom. Their English is vastly improving because I am creating an environment of immersion for them. The same goes for me. I am immersing myself in the culture and learning, but my Italian would definitely be better if I had taken some Italian language classes before moving here.

Then there's my favourite factor: the weather. I was personally tired of monotonous grey skies. The weather in the UK and Ireland was the primary factor adversely affecting my inner self. But when I moved into the wonderful and sunny atmosphere of Tuscany, everything changed. Beautiful, clear, bright and sunny skies were a wonderful reality for me, something that I had fallen in love with years before. So, do your research on the weather and see whether it is to your liking or not. Some of you may be used to sunny weather and are looking to move to places that have plenty of rainfall. It's all a matter of preference.

Next comes the cost of living. Recent research states that Ireland sits as the 5th most expensive country in Europe in which to live, with the UK in 9th position. So I have lived in places where the cost of living has been high. Now that I have moved to Italy, which lies in 15th position, the cost of living is lower and more affordable. Add into the mix that, here, the food tastes exactly as it should and is of a far superior quality. I also don't turn my heating on from April to November. So, no matter where you are from, or where you intend to move to, a vital factor is to properly evaluate how the move will impact you financially. You need to perform some serious and honest financial planning prior to booking a removal van.

There are several things that you need to ensure when it comes to financial planning. Your budget should include costs such as moving expenses, initial and continued living expenses, and emergency funds. These are fundamental to helping you survive in a completely new location abroad.

Another aspect you need to extensively research is your tax situation. What will be the tax implications of your move? It is very likely that you will have to file taxes in the country you are moving from as well as in the country you are moving to. This can be a bit confusing for most people – it certainly has been for me. I employed a good accountant (*commercialista*) and would recommend that you do the same. It's expensive, but worth it. They will walk you through everything and make it easy for you to file taxes in both countries where necessary. If the tax in the country you are moving to is significantly higher, you will have to make sure you are earning more than enough to survive.

You need to understand the local currency and what the best possible options are for you to exchange your money. Your priority should be an exchange with low fees and good exchange rates. Most of the countries across Europe that have adopted the euro freely deal in it, but if the country of your choice lies outside the EU, or if you're coming from the UK, then you can make use of this advice.

Wherever you are moving to, you need to be able to understand the healthcare system, including how to access medical services and whether you need to purchase health insurance. This is one issue you should not overlook. Your health is your greatest asset, so take good care of yourself and make sure medical aid is available to you, no matter where you move to, be it in the form of private health insurance or registering yourself in the country's universal healthcare system.

You'll need to determine whether you need a visa, and, if so, the type of visa you need. If you are moving from Ireland to the European Union, you have free movement, but, as I found out here in Italy, I still had to apply for residency to be able to do simple tasks such as buying a car. For someone moving to Italy from outwith the EU – and this now includes those coming from the UK – there are many types of visas.

Here are some:

1. Tourist Visa – This is a short-term visa for leisure in Italy. Some countries, including the UK, are exempt from the requirement to have a tourist visa. People from the exempt countries can visit visa-free for up to 90 days. Some of the requirements for this type of visa include proof of accommodation, return ticket, sufficient funds and travel insurance. There are some limitations to this type of visa, as you are not allowed to work or study.
2. Work Visa – This type of visa is for employment in the country of your choosing with an extended stay duration which varies from one to several years. It is often renewable and requires a job offer from a local employer, an employment contract, proof of qualifications and experience, and health

insurance. There is a sub-category of this type of visa called temporary work via, which is for a shorter duration and for individuals with specific skills in demand. The same kind of visa is also issued to employees transferring within the same company to a branch in the destination country.

3. Retirement Visa – This is the kind of visa for retiring in the destination country. As the name states, you are actually retiring, so you need to prove that you are retired and have sufficient retirement income to live leisurely along with health insurance, proof of property ownership or long-term rental. And since you are retired, you are not allowed to work.
4. Business Visa – This is the visa for people who intend doing some sort of business in the destination of their choosing, which may include conducting business activities such as attending meetings, conferences or exploring business opportunities. The duration for this visa varies from several days to months depending upon the nature of business. But since you are already doing business, you are not allowed to take up additional paid employment. Some of the requirements include an invitation letter from a business partner or conference organiser, proof of business activities and sufficient funds.
5. Investor or Entrepreneur Visa – This kind of visa is strictly for people who are investing in or starting a business in the destination country where the duration of the stay varies depending upon the amount of investment and is often tied to the performance of the business. Similar to the Business Visa, the requirements include proof of investment funds, a business plan, proof of business ownership or significant investment, and health insurance.
6. Permanent Residency Visa – This visa means you are applying to become a permanent resident of the destination country. If your application is successful, your duration is indefinite, but

only after holding a temporary visa for a certain period of time. The requirements vary greatly from one country to another – usually long-term residency, proof of stable income, integration into the community and a clean criminal record. Two types of permanent residency visas include Family-based Permanent Residency and Employment-based Permanent Residency.

7. Italy has just introduced (April 2024) a Nomad Visa, where a non-EU remote worker can apply to remain in the country initially for one year, but that can be extended. You have to operate as an employee or consultant working remotely.

So, if a visa is required, you will have to opt for the one that fits your needs. If you're going to a country for a dry run to figure out compatibility, then I recommend a tourist visa, but if you need to find employment in the country of choice, then a work or business visa will do. If you have a significant amount of funds available, then your best choice would be an investor or entrepreneur visa. All in all, research the one that fits your needs.

Once you have figured out the right kind of visa you need, or if you are already from the EU, where no visa is required, you will have to apply for the residency permit. I know the multiple hoops I went through to get my residency permit. Initially upon arrival you should register with the local authority so that they know you are here. They will give you an application and show you the administrative challenges that lie ahead. Italians are known for over-administering everything – and I have certainly found that to be the case – but a residency permit is a must.

Driving: the first thing you must do is check if your current driver's licence is valid in your new country. It may be, but it might not be, or it may lapse after a certain period of grace time. It's something you need to figure out by reaching out to the authorities. If it's not valid, you'll need to obtain an international driving permit or a local licence. This may not be that important if you are moving to a large city, where you can take whatever transport the locals use to commute, which could vary from stuffed buses to an overly crowded metro. In rural Tuscany, a car is a must.

Accommodation: I bought my apartment years before moving here permanently. If you are just sticking your toe in the water, you should consider renting first. Have a good look around, get a feel for the place and then, further down the line, if the place is for you, start looking to buy a property.

In case you opt for the long-term rental market, then be sure to read the lease agreement, and get into that fine text. If you're moving to an area that has hordes of tourists in the summer, make sure the lease agreement doesn't require that you leave in June so that the landlord can take advantage of higher holiday rentals.

Utilities: gas, electricity, water, mobile network and internet, all of which you cannot survive without. Some places already have those set up, especially if you are renting; however, if you have bought your own place and have no utilities, you'll need to reach out to the local service providers and have them installed. The sooner you get them, the better for you. Monthly costs of these services in Italy are virtually identical to those in the UK and Ireland.

All of the aforementioned steps and factors are essential, and I speak from experience when I tell you how meticulous you need to be when it comes to preparing – particularly financially – and having an escape plan/pot.

So, once you have completed your research and planning, it's time to pack and start shipping. This step is optional if you don't want to take anything with you. I sold and gave away 98% of what I owned. If you do need to ship your goods, you must first declutter to decide what you want to take and what you are going to leave behind. Whatever remains, you can either sell, donate or simply discard. The less you move with, the less stress you carry along. Since you are shipping your possessions, do a little research on shipping companies and compare quotes. Reach out to the top- to middle-tier service providers only, and make sure they offer insurance. See what options are available to you, such as sea or air. Air shipping is faster, but it's expensive compared to sea. Factor in the cost and delivery time and decide which option suits you best. Pack everything securely. Make sure to label boxes and use lots of packing foam for fragile items.

As for your documents, such as passports, visas, birth certificates, financial records, etc., keep them in a secure and accessible place during the move. If you are alone, then having them in a closely held bag or a crossbody shoulder bag is a good idea. In case you are with family, you can have a backpack and have everything in it. Photograph all of these documents as a backup.

Once there, start by registering with the local authorities. Register with the healthcare providers and familiarise yourself with the local medical facilities – what is the local emergency numbers for the police/fire brigade/ambulance? Get your utilities and banking set up, and then you can try to integrate into the community by getting involved in local activities. Meet up with social groups and local people in an attempt to develop a social circle of your own. Remember, this is very difficult if you cannot speak the local language, but persevere.

Moving doesn't mean you shouldn't maintain contact with your friends and family. I started my TikTok account #OldManAbroad only because I wanted to keep my children updated on how I was doing. You can do it too. Make a channel on YouTube, TikTok, Facebook or Instagram to keep your friends and family updated on how you are getting on. With the progress of technology, we now have the power to reach the other end of the world in an instant via a video call. Staying connected with them is not just for their sake but also for your own emotional well-being.

Finally, stay positive. Moving abroad is not a small change in life; it is perhaps the biggest change you can make, apart from becoming a parent. Nonetheless, it is an opportunity for you to learn and grow.

Chapter 21
'You Bought What !!!!! ?'

I used to own one of the tallest grandfather clocks in the world: the Portrush Railway Station Grandfather Clock. I had zero intention of being a clock owner, wasn't particularly interested in clocks and wasn't even aware that Portrush Railway Station had an internal grandfather clock. The following, and first couple of pages of this chapter, is the official version of the description of the clock. The background story of its ownership is a wee bit more colourful.

> The Portrush Railway Station in Northern Ireland was notable for its historic grandfather clock, believed to be one of the tallest free-standing clocks in the world. Commissioned in 1892, the clock stands approximately 17.5 feet tall and features two faces, each three feet in diameter. It was crafted by Sharman D. Neill, a renowned Belfast clockmaker of the Victorian era.
>
> Originally installed in the General Hall of Portrush Railway Station, the clock was a central feature for travellers, symbolising the importance of time in railway travel. It remained there until the early 1970s when it was removed during station refurbishments. In 2004, local resident Barry Torrens purchased the clock to prevent it from being sold overseas and lost to the local community, ensuring it remained on the north coast.
>
> After years without a permanent home, the clock was acquired in 2024 by C&V Developments Ltd, the company behind the newly approved £20 million Merrow Hotel & Spa development in Portstewart. The developers plan to feature the clock prominently within the hotel, preserving this significant piece of local

heritage for both residents and visitors to appreciate.

The clock has witnessed over a century of history, from Queen Victoria's reign through two world wars and the partition of Ireland. Its preservation within the Merrow Hotel & Spa ensures that it will continue to be a cherished symbol of the area's rich cultural heritage.

The display on the plinth in front of the clock said the following:

I am the Portrush Railway Station Grandfather Clock. I was made in 1892 by the renowned clockmaker Sharman D. Neill, Belfast, and I am reputed to be the tallest free-standing grandfather clock in the world, standing a proud 5.5 metres tall. I was erected in Portrush Railway Station in 1892 when Queen Victoria was Monarch, and I stood between the platforms until about 1975. During that period, I witnessed many of the events that have shaped our lives today.

In 1912 I was merely 20 years old when news broke of the tragic loss of life during the ill-fated maiden voyage of the Belfast ship R.M.S. Titanic.

In 1914 I watched as the gallant young volunteers left from this area in trains for the front lines and trenches of northern France to fight in the 'Great War for Civilisation' and witnessed with a sad heart as a small number of those men returned 4 years later from a war that was described as the 'War to end all Wars'.

In 1939 I watched again as men from this area left Portrush Railway Station for the Second World War and I welcomed the American G.I.s that arrived and trained around the North Coast preparing themselves for a final assault on the occupying forces of Nazi Germany. I watched with joy in June 1945 as the people of Portrush celebrated VE Day and then VJ day in

August of that year. Boy, they knew how to party!

I watched as Ireland was partitioned in 1921 and Northern Ireland was born. Today, I am in the fortunate position to witness the peace that is being enjoyed by the people seeking the time that I display.

Alongside these historic events, I watched the hundreds of thousands of excited holiday makers arrive and then depart over the decades, coming to Portrush to bathe in the sea, play on our beautiful beaches and of course parade their Sunday best along the promenades. Who knows, I may have watched as your Great Great Great Grandfather and Great Great Great Grandmother strolled arm in arm.

In 1994 I was found in a reclamation yard, and I was nearly used as a climbing frame for the chimpanzees in the old Causeway Safari Park near Ballybogey. Thank heavens I was saved from that fate. Recently, I was sold to an international antiques dealer who had found a buyer for me in the USA, and I was awaiting shipment in a port in England when I was bought and returned to Portrush by the Torrens family. I have recently been restored, and I now stand on the North Coast again where I have displayed the time since the 19th century.

In my 133 years I have been many colours, including natural wood, cream, black, white and even purple, each generation adding their own distinctive style.

Thankfully I am able to stand here today due to the determination and support of a large number of individuals who share the same passion in, and dedication to, our wonderful North Coast.

Now for another version. In 2004 I was happily living in Portrush on the north coast of Northern Ireland. The beautiful property my wife and I bought was a mere 5 metres from the sea and had a stunning outlook across the north coast along beautiful sandy beaches, white cliffs, Dunluce Castle and beyond to the world heritage site that is the Giant's Causeway. We were enormously happy and at that stage we had two infant daughters (my son was still to be born) and I was daily travelling to Belfast as a working barrister-at-law.

I have always had an interest in the local north coast community and also generally in history, so when an article was published in the local newspaper, *The Coleraine Times*, edited during this period by David Rankin, it caught my eye. The frontpage headline said something along the lines, 'Can we save our heritage?' Reading deeper, the story continued that a grandfather clock that used to stand for nearly 100 years on the train platform of Portrush Railway Station had been transported to Heysham Port near Liverpool and was about to be shipped to the USA. The paper was attempting to campaign to ensure the clock would be returned to Portrush, as it was an important historic artefact for the local and wider community. They had already approached the local council, who responded by understanding the significance of the artefact, but they could not afford to purchase the clock. The newspaper's frontpage campaign, that ran over a number of weeks, attempted to garner support for the council to step in.

During this time, I spoke to my then wife about the clock and how I thought it was an awful shame that not only specifically Portrush/the north coast was losing the clock, but also that Northern Ireland was losing a piece of history. I understood and still understand that others might think nothing of losing parts of our heritage, but to me every loss is a chipping away at our identity and one day, in the not-too-distant future, we could look up and find everything will be made of concrete, soulless and uninspiring, and items like this clock will be lost forever. So, bearing this in mind, I kept an eye on the newspaper campaign. Following week – no buyer. Then, it's leaving soon for the USA – no buyer. I spoke to my wife again saying how poor this would be to see this piece lost, but she didn't have anywhere near the same enthusiasm for such artefacts or for the story.

I decided to ask a few more questions than what was being provided by the paper, so I contacted the editor. David came back with more information and contact details of the seller of the clock. Sure, it wouldn't do any harm to ask for some details about the clock from the owner and what realistic price he was seeking to return the clock to Portrush. The owner told me he had a buyer for the clock in Florida, USA, specifically a golf course. I wasn't and I'm not aware whether this was true. I wasn't the slightest bit interested in this information, only whether he would consider returning the clock to Northern Ireland. He quoted a price that would choke an elephant, so I put two hands up, thanked him for his time and ended the conversation. I resigned myself to the fact that the clock would disappear. A few days later I received further correspondence stating a very different price that tweaked my interest. I replied offering a fraction of the new price, and he walked away. Four days later he contacted me again stating a new price that was very close to my last offer … deal done. I was now the owner of the tallest grandfather clock in the world. Oookaayy.

Now what do I do? Hmm, importantly, I needed to tell my wife, as she had zero enthusiasm for this story. Prior to this difficult conversation – which I knew might be a bit awkward – my wife had taken a trip to the local corner shop for milk and bread. She returned with a small bag of groceries and a newspaper, *The Coleraine Times*. The headline in the paper that day was 'Clock Saved for Local Community'. Opening the folded paper, she read this headline and said, 'Ha, Barry, you don't have to worry about that clock, some prat has bought it.' And she continued reading: 'The Portrush Railway Station Grandfather Clock has been saved and will return to the north coast following a campaign by this newspaper. Local businessman Barry Torrens stepped in and purchased …'. That's the last words I heard my wife say for about three months – all pictures and no sound in my house. Eeek.

Apart from zero interest about this clock within my household, the clock returning was greeted with enthusiasm in the wider community. This nearly 6 metre clock arrived back to Portrush after being away for many years. The return made the news, and this event was published in the GB press as well as being widely reported throughout Northern Ireland. I purchased the clock on three conditions that I set for myself: (i) it would be working, (ii) it would remain on the north coast and (iii) it would be on public display. So, I set about ensuring these conditions were met. I needed joiners for the wood, welders for the metal, a horologist (clockmaker), painters, forklift and driver, and a removals team to move it around. I employed every one of these individuals on a commercial basis and reached payment to them when they had finished their respective jobs. Everyone, bar none, refused payment. Some were entitled to hundreds of pounds, but, because I had purchased the clock to return it to Portrush for the local community, each of them separately and individually refused to accept one penny in payment. I was deeply touched by that and will always remember it.

Once renovations were complete, the next step was housing the clock – not an easy prospect as it is nearly 6 metres tall. There are very few buildings that can accept this piece, but also permit it to be on public display. The council told me they couldn't help, so I had a look around. We had and still have a large indoor amusement park in Portrush. It used to be called Barry's Amusements. I actually worked there as a boy during my school summer holidays. I approached the owners – a lovely north coast family – to see whether they would be able to help display the clock. The patriarch and lovely gentleman, the late Frank Trufelli, happily agreed to display the clock on a temporary basis until I could find a permanent location. Barry's kept the clock in situ. for some eight years. It was a perfect place for the clock, as it stood merely 80 metres away from where it had stood for nearly 100 years. The old train station was now in private hands and could not accommodate it.

I then moved the clock to the council chambers where it still stands today. When my children moved away from the area and I emigrated to Italy, I put the clock up for sale, having owned it for nearly 20 years. It went up for sale on the same conditions I had imposed on myself: (i) it would be working, (ii) it would remain on the north coast and (iii) it would be on public display. I was approached by another lovely individual who was in the process of building a hotel on the north coast, and she purchased it. I refused to make one penny profit on the clock and sold it for what I had bought it for. It will eventually be moved and displayed when the new hotel is built on the north coast. Job done.

Chapter 22
Adventure

Adventure, for me, has always been more than just an act of exploration and travelling. It's a mindset that shapes how you experience the world, how you approach challenges and how you view yourself. From the moment I stepped into the unknown, from the first plane flight to the first mountain summit, I understood that adventure wasn't simply about the places you visit or the things you accomplish. It was about pushing beyond the boundaries of what you think you're capable of, leaving the comfort of the familiar behind and stepping out. Every new experience brings with it the opportunity for growth, not just physically but spiritually and mentally. When climbing Mont Blanc, I felt the world was below me, and only space was above. On summit day I had a few frightening experiences, but it taught me to push past my fears when faced with the unknown. It taught me resilience, patience, determination and humility.

I've travelled to various countries across the globe, each one teaching me something different, each journey offering a new perspective. I've roamed through the misty peaks of Peru, experienced the chaos of Nepal and wandered the ancient streets of Rome. In each of these places, I was both an outsider and a participant, discovering not just new landscapes but new ways of seeing the world. These journeys forced me to face discomfort and uncertainty and to learn from it. I realised that it is in the discomfort, in the moments when everything feels unfamiliar, that your mind and body adapt, and that is when we grow the most. Recording these trips for my children has become a way for me to share the spirit of adventure that has fuelled my life, inviting them into the world I've discovered, and perhaps inspiring them to seek out their own paths of exploration.

And now, living in Italy, I've come to realise that adventure isn't just about travelling to far-off places, but about embracing life wherever you are. Tuscany, with its quiet and rolling hills, has shown me that adventure can exist in the simplest of moments. Whether it's walking through the streets of Montaione, hiking up a quiet hill to watch the sun set over the valley or immersing myself in the deep traditions of local culture, I have found that every new experience here holds the potential for profound transformation. It's the adventure of slowing down, of truly living in the present, and of connecting deeply with both the land and the people.

Every adventure, whether small or large, has the power to change us, to challenge us and to open up new possibilities in our lives. The world is full of opportunities for growth and discovery, but we must be willing to take that first step. It's easy to get stuck in the safety of routine, to stay within the boundaries of what we know, but it's in pushing those boundaries that we find our true potential. It's absolutely fine if you are a person who cannot or does not want to step outside your comfort zone. This book isn't a lecture; it's merely a peek into my world where I like to, and want to, push myself and experience what is unknown to me.

Adventure, for me, has always been a guiding force, something that has shaped not only my life but my understanding of the world. There is power in exploration, in venturing out into the unknown, that goes beyond the physical act of travelling. An adventure can be found in education, a new job, a new town or a new business. Each journey I've undertaken has been more than just a trip; it's been a transformative experience, a chance to stretch my limits, challenge my assumptions, and I've grown in ways I could never have imagined.

My geographical travels have taken me to places that have changed me, places that have tested my courage and expanded my perspective. I think about trekking in the mountains of Nepal pre-earthquakes, where every step felt like a test of both physical endurance and mental fortitude. The air was thin, the terrain harsh and the journey long, but with each day, I found myself not only growing stronger physically but also discovering new depths of resilience. There's something about being so far from civilisation that makes you confront your own limitations, and in doing so, you discover how much further you can go than you ever thought possible. It was in Nepal that I realised how adventure isn't just about the external physical journey, but also about the internal shifts that take place, the quiet moments of thought when you're miles away from your comfort zone and forced to look inward.

Peru taught me about the power of history, of ancient civilisations that have shaped the land and its people. It also taught me something about myself. Walking those ancient Incan paths, I felt a deep sense of connection to the people who constructed the thousands of kilometres of walkways. It wasn't just the physical beauty that was transformative, but also the sense of awe that came from stepping into a place so rich with history. Summitting Mont Blanc was a culmination of nearly a year of training and mental preparation. Reaching the summit wasn't just about standing on top of a mountain, but about pushing through the moments of doubt, fear, the times when every muscle in my body screamed for rest. Mont Blanc was a test of my limits, a reminder that growth often happens at the edge of discomfort. As an aside, the specialist high altitude boots I was wearing for this climb had a pinhole puncture in the right boot. My big toe on my right foot froze and lost all feeling. I never regained the feeling and can still feel the effects of Mont Blanc summit day on my right big toe over ten years later.

Each of these adventures taught me more about myself than any classroom ever could. They showed me the power of exploration, not just the act of discovering new places, but the power of expanding my perspective and of challenging the limits I had placed on myself. The lessons learned on these journeys are ones that will stay with me forever, shaping my understanding of life and myself. Sometimes, it's just about taking the first step. It's okay to feel uncertain, to feel the fear, but to push forward anyway. The beauty of adventure is that it's not reserved for the brave, the young or the reckless. Adventure is for anyone who has the courage to embrace it. It's for those who are willing to take the first step, no matter how small, and venture into the unknown.

Each new journey I undertook forced me to reframe how I saw myself. I learned that I am capable of more than I thought possible, that my limits are self-imposed, and that stepping outside of them reveals parts of myself I didn't even know existed. Even in the quieter moments – such as strolling through the markets in a small village or sitting by the sea on a remote island – adventure forced me to slow down and truly see the world and myself. I began to realise how much of our daily lives are filled with distractions, and how much we miss when we don't take the time to reflect. Adventure gave me the space to do that, to reconnect with my inner self and to find clarity in chaos. I've come to understand that life is not a linear path. It's filled with moments of clarity, moments of confusion and, most importantly, moments of profound growth.

When I first arrived here, I wasn't sure what to expect. The landscape, with its beauty, has a way of calling you to slow down, to breathe and to simply be. There is an almost meditative quality to the land here. The serenity of the countryside offers a sense of peace that is hard to find anywhere else. It was here, among the vineyards of Montaione and the cobbled streets of small Tuscan towns, that I began to understand the true meaning of living. Tuscany has taught me that sometimes the greatest adventure is not in conquering distant lands but in embracing the stillness, the simplicity and the quiet joy of being fully present in your surroundings.

Chapter 23
Wine Festival and 'Just Dad'

Meeting and speaking with the locals here, I have come to appreciate food and wine to a level I never considered before. Before I moved to Italy, food and wine were just pastimes I didn't think about too deeply. Wine was merely a drink to help me relax or to enjoy when out with friends. But in Italy, it's more than just a drink. Here, wine represents all the different places it comes from. These small localities produce a variety of different types of wines, each with its own distinct flavour and aroma. Every wine has its own tale to tell: its origin, how it got to you, and what it will offer you aside from a massive hangover if you are not too careful with it. I went to a local wine festival here, the Borgo D'Avino festival, which had set up in my town, bringing with it wine producers from every region.

I arrived early, around half seven, to avoid the throngs that would inevitably show up later. The previous night had been packed, so for my visit I planned to beat the crowd. The festival didn't officially kick off until nine, so I had plenty of time to explore the producers' stalls at my leisure.

As I wandered around, I noticed there were about forty wine producers set up, each offering a unique selection. From Piedmont to Sardinia, Tuscany to Emilia Romagna, the variety was amazing. Everywhere I turned, there were familiar faces who greeted me warmly. Tuscany's wines, especially Chianti, have always been my favourite. I started my evening with a glass from Castelfalfi, a high-end resort's offering. This Chianti was pure Sangiovese, a whopping 14% alcohol, and cost €65 a bottle – way out of my price range, but it was a treat to taste such an exquisite wine. Moving on, I tried wines priced at €32, then €20 per bottle. Each sip was delicious, though I firmly believe you don't need to exceed €15 to enjoy a good Chianti. The atmosphere was buzzing. The church bells rang in the background, children ran around playing and families gathered under the still-shining sun, enjoying the festive spirit.

The festival had a romantic vibe that night, being dubbed the 'night of lovers.' I roamed through the crowd, making mental notes of the wines I enjoyed. My palate leaned towards full-bodied reds. Wine tasting is a personal experience, and what I love might not be someone else's cup of tea. One standout for me was the Chianti from the Tognetti vineyard at Podere la Casetta, just outside Montaione. Their wines, priced between €8 and €14, were a revelation. The blend of 75% or 100% Sangiovese grapes produced a wine that was both affordable and exceptional. It was, without doubt, the highlight of my evening.

When I first heard about Borgo D'Avino, I had no idea what to expect. A travelling wine festival sounded intriguing, but the reality exceeded my expectations. The festival had an energy that was infectious. The sheer variety of wines on offer was wonderful, from robust reds to crisp whites, there was something for every palate.

I spent a good chunk of my evening chatting with the producers. These weren't just vendors, but passionate artisans who poured their hearts and souls into their wines. They shared stories of their vineyards, the grape varieties they used and the meticulous process of winemaking. It was fascinating to hear about the history and tradition behind each bottle. One producer from Sardinia, for example, told me about the unique challenges of growing grapes on the island. The climate, the soil and even the sea breeze all played a role in shaping the flavour of their wines. I tried a Vermentino that was like nothing I'd ever tasted before – crisp, fresh, with a hint of the sea.

As the night wore on, the festival became busier. More people arrived, and the air was filled with laughter and lively conversation. I ran into some friends, and we decided to sample a few more wines together. We made our way to a stall from Emilia Romagna, where they were pouring a sparkling red that was absolutely delightful. It was light and bubbly, perfect for the warm evening. One of my favourite encounters was with a producer from Veneto. They had a selection of Amarone wines that were rich and complex. I had a conversation with the winemaker about the ageing process and how it affected the flavour profile. I could taste the years of care and attention that had gone into each bottle.

The festival wasn't just about the wine, though. There was a sense of community and celebration that permeated the air. People were genuinely happy to be there, sharing in the joy of good wine and good company. By the end of the night, I had tasted many wines. My favourite was still the Chianti from Podere la Casetta. The combination of affordability and quality was unbeatable. With the equivalent of four glasses of various reds swirling pleasantly in my system and a fine cigar to cap off the night, I decided it was time to call it a day. The festival would carry on into the wee hours, but I had reached my limit. As the sun dipped lower and the festival grew busier, I left, content and slightly tipsy. As I made my way home, I couldn't help but feel grateful for the experience. Borgo D'Avino had introduced me not only to some fantastic wines but also to the people and stories behind them. It was a reminder of why I loved Italy so much: the rich culture, the warm people and, of course, the incredible wine.

For those of you who have been following my journey and watching my videos, you'll know that I moved to Italy because I wanted to live somewhere where I could enjoy, mostly, blue skies and sunshine. When my youngest headed off to university, it meant all three of my children were then in university across England and Scotland.

My children are amazing, wonderful and respectful. But during my recent trip to visit them, I noticed something that I had tentatively recognised when I was with them the previous Christmas. I used to be the centre of their world. Being a dad was my greatest role, and I threw myself into it completely. I was the entertainer, the disciplinarian, the driver, the educator, the adviser, the safety guy – all of that and more. I absolutely loved it.

Now, though, watching them spread their wings and fly, becoming beautiful young adults themselves, I realise that I am now just a bit player in their lives. I'm no longer a central character. It's a natural progression, I know, but coming to terms with it has been tough. These days, I'm someone they chat with once a week on FaceTime and text daily. But my role has changed. I'm no longer the one they rely on for most things, and that's been hard to accept. If you don't have children, it might be difficult to understand. Even if you do have children but they live close by, you might not fully grasp what I'm feeling. But as an empty-nester, I'm finding the realisation difficult and heartbreaking.

My children couldn't be more loving, but the shift in my role has been profound. If I'd stayed in Northern Ireland under those grey skies, I don't know how I would've managed this transition. Here in Italy, the sunshine helps. For me, lying in the sun for an hour feels like an injection of happiness. But even with the sunny days, this past week has been bittersweet. It was lovely to see my children, but also heartbreaking because I realised I'm not needed in the same way anymore. Instead of being their everything, I'm now 'just Dad'. For someone who thrived on being a father, this has been a tough adjustment. Tuscany has been a balm for my soul, with its beauty and warmth offering some comfort as I navigate this new phase of life.

Returning to my little garden here in Montaione, I find some solace in caring for my plants. They depend on me, and, in a small way, it brings back a sense of being needed. Plus, there's something therapeutic about tending to the earth and watching things grow under the Tuscan sun. My children are off building their own lives, and I'm here, building a new chapter in mine. It's not what I expected, and it's certainly not always easy, but I'm learning to embrace it. This move to Italy has been a blessing in disguise, helping me find joy in the little things and reminding me that life is full of unexpected turns.

I made a TikTok video about being 'just Dad', and when my

children saw it, they sent me a wonderful card that warmed my heart.

It said:

> To the BEST Dad ever,
>
> We will ALWAYS need you, no matter how far away we are from each other. We all miss you loads. You are not, just Dad – you are our HERO.
>
> See you soon.
>
> Lots and lots of love,
> Penster, Banana, and Big Bad Bill XOX

I wonder how they will react to me adding my nicknames for them here. In case you guys are reading it, sorry, but couldn't help myself.

On one of my visits to the UK, seven people came up to me to say hello because they recognised me as the Old Man Abroad from my videos. It was heartwarming. So, if you do see me, please feel free to come up and say hello. Just a small request, though: when you come up to say hi, please tell me how you know me. I'd be delighted to meet you and say hello.

In addition to maintaining the small Toscana English Academy, I have just started inviting people to visit and showing them around this enchanting area. When my guests arrive, we explore Pisa, Florence, San Gimignano, Peccioli and sometimes Volterra. We visit places like the Teatro del Silenzio and San Vivaldo. I take them to my favourite spots, we enjoy the delicious Italian food, and it's always a fabulous time. If you're interested in the itinerary, just have a look at www.sunflower-bellissima-toscana.com. Feel free to send me a message or ask any questions you have.

Living alone in Tuscany this past year has had its challenges, but it's also been a journey of self-discovery. The beautiful landscape, the rich culture and the wonderful people I've met along the way have made it all worthwhile. For now, I'm focusing on enjoying my life here, meeting new people and sharing the beauty of Tuscany with my visitors. I've realised that life has many phases, and each one brings its own set of joys and challenges. Moving to Tuscany has been a big change, but it has also been incredibly fulfilling. I've found new ways to connect with people. The friendships I've built and the experiences I've had are invaluable. Every day here is a new adventure, whether I'm exploring a new part of Tuscany, meeting visitors or simply tending to my terrace. The slower pace of life has given me the chance to appreciate the little things and find contentment in everyday moments. For now, I'm happy and I'm looking forward to what each new day brings in this beautiful corner of the world.

Chapter 24
Did I Do the Right Thing?

On 6th July 2023, I stood on the promenade of my hometown, staring at the horizon. The wind was strong and biting, the rain coming down almost sideways, and the waves crashing harder than I'd seen for a long time. I wasn't sure if it was the weather or my mood, but everything felt heavier that day. The kind of heavy that clings to your bones and refuses to let go.

My children, my anchors for so long, were now off living their own lives – university, careers, independence. I was proud of them, of course, but their absence left an emptiness I couldn't quite fill. That day wasn't just about the weather or turning 53. It was about a kind of reckoning. I stood there, soaked to the skin, feeling as if the world was asking: 'What's next? What are you waiting for?' … And for the first time, I didn't have an answer.

I thought about my parents and grandparents, who had lived their whole lives in Northern Ireland. They had settled into the same routines, the same streets, the same skies. It wasn't a bad life, but it wasn't the life I wanted for myself, not now. They had their reasons for staying; I had mine for leaving. I'd been thinking about leaving for a while – years if I'm being honest. But there's always something to keep you rooted – responsibilities, children, the fear of the unknown. But as I stood there, the rain soaking through my coat, the thought came to me more clearly than ever … 'Why not now?'

It wasn't some dramatic moment of clarity. It wasn't cinematic. It was just practical. My children didn't need me in the same way anymore. The house was empty. The life I'd built had run its course. And I knew that if I didn't make a go of it now, I never would. Of course, the idea of leaving wasn't without its doubts. What if I failed? What if the new place wasn't what I'd imagined? What if this whole idea was just a midlife crisis wrapped in a plane ticket? But as I stood there, I realised the bigger risk was staying – staying in a place that no longer felt like home, living a life that no longer felt like mine.

It's strange how you can spend decades building something – family, career, a sense of stability – and then, in one rain-soaked moment, realise you're ready to leave it all behind. That's what happened to me that day, just over a year ago. It wasn't about running away. It was about running towards something, even if I didn't fully know what that something was yet. And so, that's how it began – not with fireworks or fanfare, but with rain and resolve. I didn't have all the answers. I didn't even know all the questions. But I knew one thing for sure – it was time to go.

Deciding to leave was one thing; actually leaving was another. Once the idea took root, the practicalities of it started weighing on me. How do you dismantle a life you've spent decades building? Where do you even begin? I started with the obvious: the things I didn't need – furniture, old electronics, clothes I hadn't worn in 12 months. It wasn't hard to let those go. I donated some, sold others and gave away what I could to friends and charity. But then came the harder decisions, the things that weren't just things.

My shelves were filled with books I'd read to my children at bedtime, the walls held photographs from family holidays and the cupboards were crammed with art projects and keepsakes that no one had looked at in years but somehow felt impossible to part with. As I sorted through it all, I realised how much of myself was tied up in these objects. I wasn't just packing boxes; I was sorting through memories. Each item I touched brought back a moment in time – a birthday party, an adventure, a Christmas morning. It was overwhelming at times, but also grounding. These weren't just remnants of the past, but pieces of a story I was proud to have lived.

When it came to the more meaningful items, the decision became clearer. I didn't want to take them with me, not because they didn't matter, but because they did. They belonged to my children now, as much a part of their history as mine. So, I started dividing them up: a sentimental diamond ring for my eldest, my Olympic Torch for my middle child and my grandfather's WW1 and WW2 medals for my son. It felt less like saying goodbye and more like passing them on for safe keeping. It wasn't about the monetary value of these items, but about the stories they carried. Handing these over wasn't just practical; it was symbolic. It was my way of telling them, this is where we've come from, this is who we are, and now it's yours to carry forward.

Packing the small amount of things I was taking felt sad – is this what I've amounted to, a small carload? But then I understood that this was my choice to live an uncluttered life, and I have come to enjoy it. Leaving wasn't just about starting over, but about closing a chapter, and, as I handed over the keys, I felt lighter – not because I was letting go of the past, but because I was making room for the future. The memories didn't need a particular house to exist. They were with me and always would be.

Moving to another country is exciting, yes, but it's also chaotic. The paperwork – residency permits, tax codes, health insurance – which I can only describe as a labyrinth designed to test every ounce of patience I possessed, all had to be done, and all of it in a language I didn't understand. The officials were kind enough, but their speed was often … leisurely. I quickly learned that *domani*, or tomorrow, doesn't always mean tomorrow. Sometimes it means next week, or go away. In the middle of the bureaucratic madness, there were moments that reminded me why I'd come. My first trip to the local market was overwhelming in the best way. Vendors shouted greetings, their stalls bursting with fresh produce, bread and cheeses that seemed too perfect to eat. I remember fumbling through a transaction, mixing up the words for various fruits – and instead of frustration, the vendor laughed, patted my arm and corrected me with a smile.

The hospitality didn't stop there. My neighbours introduced themselves within days, offering any form of assistance as if we'd known each other for years. One even invited me over for dinner, and I soon found myself sitting at a table groaning under the weight of pasta, wine and endless conversation. I didn't understand much of what was being said, but it didn't matter. The warmth in the room, hand signals and smiles are universal.

Of course, there were surprises, too. Italians love their routines, and the local café became a lesson in cultural immersion. Cappuccinos are strictly for the morning. Ordering one after noon earned me a gentle shake of the head and a patient explanation of proper coffee etiquette. Supermarkets closed for hours in the afternoon, and driving was less about rules and more about instinct, luck and prayer. Still, with every misstep, every laughable mistake, Italy began to feel a little more like home. The chaos of the arrival gradually gave way to something quieter – a rhythm I hadn't yet mastered but was starting to understand. I wasn't just visiting Italy; I was becoming part of it.

Settling in is one thing, but building a life here is another. The first and main challenge was obvious – I needed to learn the language. Italian is beautiful, musical even, but when you're trying to wrap your head around verbs that seem to change form every other sentence, it's not quite so poetic. I downloaded apps, bought textbooks and practised with YouTube videos, but nothing prepared me for real conversations. Italians speak with a speed and passion that left me scrambling to catch a single word, let alone understand a full sentence.

Early on, I ventured to the butcher's shop, armed with the phrase I'd practised repeatedly: *Vorrei un chilo di carne macinata, per favore.* I wanted minced meat. Simple enough, I thought, but as soon as the words left my mouth, the butcher launched into a stream of rapid Italian, and started asking me something I couldn't begin to decipher. I stared blankly and said '*Sì*' and left with a bag of something that definitely wasn't minced meat. Humility became my constant companion. Every mistake, every mix-up, became a story to laugh about later. My Italian friends were endlessly patient, though. They'd correct me with a kind smile or, when it was really hopeless, just ask me to speak in English. 'Barry, Barry, please, just English,' they'd say, laughing. Still, bit by bit, the words came. I found joy in small victories, successfully asking for directions, or ordering a meal without needing to mime. It wasn't perfect, and it never will be, but it was progress.

While I wrestled with the language, I also had to figure out how to make a living. I couldn't just drift along indefinitely. Starting a small business in a foreign country isn't exactly straightforward – a mountain of more paperwork, more waiting – but when the doors finally opened, I felt a sense of accomplishment I hadn't felt in years. Teaching English brought a purpose to my days. My students ranged from eager smiling children to retirees who wanted to travel more. There was something fulfilling about seeing their progress, hearing them piece together sentences they didn't think they could say. It wasn't just about teaching a language, but also about building connections. And those connections extended beyond the classroom. The local community embraced me in ways I hadn't expected. But it wasn't, and still isn't, easy. There were and are moments of loneliness. Living in a place where you don't understand the language or customs is isolating, even when surrounded by people.

Italy doesn't move at the same pace as the UK, and that's not a bad thing. It forced me to slow down, to let go of the urgency I'd been carrying for years. Life here has its own rhythm – one I'm still learning to dance to. Little by little, I'm building a life. A life where currently the challenges are part of the story, not the whole of it. A life filled with new friends, new routines, new dreams. A life I couldn't have imagined when I stood on that rainy promenade back home. And perhaps that's the greatest lesson of all. Sometimes, starting over isn't about erasing the past. It's about adding to it, piece by piece, until it becomes something you never thought possible.

A few weeks ago, I was sitting in my quiet Italian apartment one evening, thinking about the stormy day back in Northern Ireland when this journey began. Although only a year had passed, it seemed to me like a lifetime ago. At 53, I hadn't just decided to move; I'd decided to change everything. But change isn't easy. It's uncomfortable, unpredictable and, at times, terrifying. But the thought that kept coming back to me was this: if not now, when? Life doesn't stretch endlessly ahead of us, no matter how much we'd like to believe it does. I had spent years watching my parents and grandparents live out their later years in the same places, doing the same things. It worked for them, but it wasn't what I wanted for myself.

By my reckoning, I have maybe 20 good years left, years where I'll still have the energy to explore, to try new things, to learn and to grow. Beyond that, who knows? I'm not afraid of getting older, but I don't want to wait until the opportunities I've craved slip out of reach. My window to live boldly is small, and I don't want to waste it. That sense of urgency was what pushed me forward to a life filled with sunshine, curiosity and possibility. The idea of staying, of settling into a routine that no longer fulfilled me, felt like a slow erosion of everything I wanted to be. I didn't want to wake up one day, years later, and realise I'd missed my chance.

The move to Italy taught me more than I ever expected. First and foremost, it taught me about fear, how it whispers every reason you shouldn't do something, how it keeps you in place with the promise of safety. But safety isn't the same as happiness, and staying still isn't the same as living. Every fear I faced in making this move – fear of failure, loneliness or not fitting in – was outweighed by the rewards of stepping into the unknown. It also taught me about courage. Not the loud, dramatic kind of courage, but the quiet, steady kind that gets you through one small challenge at a time. Courage, I realised, isn't the absence of fear, but the decision to act despite it. Each time I tackled a new challenge, from navigating Italian bureaucracy to building a business, I proved to myself that I could do it. And with each success, the next challenge seemed a little less daunting.

Finally, this journey has taught me the value of saying yes. Yes to the unfamiliar, yes to the difficult, yes to the life I wanted but didn't fully know how to achieve. The act of saying yes – to moving, to learning, to starting over – opened doors I hadn't even known existed. Looking back, the decision to change wasn't just about moving to

Italy; it was about embracing the idea that life is fluid, that it's never too late to add to your story. That realisation didn't come all at once, but as I reflect now, it's clear that the greatest risk wasn't leaving. The greatest risk would have been staying.

Now, my life in Italy is unhurried, deliberate and steeped in simple pleasures. My days are filled with small moments that I once might have overlooked but which now feel like the very essence of living. Morning walks through cobbled streets have become a ritual, where I'm greeted with '*Buongiorno*' at every turn. It's not just the scenery or the festivals that make my life special here; it's the mindset it has given me. I've learned to savour these moments without rushing to the next thing. I've learned to sit with a coffee in the afternoon, watching the world go by, without feeling the need to fill the silence with activity. More than anything, I'm grateful. Grateful that I made the leap, grateful for the people who've welcomed me here, and grateful for the chance to wake up each day in a place that feels like life.

Life is short, and quick. Staying safe and comfortable might feel easier, but it won't always bring you joy. If it suits you and you want to, take the risk, step into the unknown. The reward isn't just in what you find, but also in discovering what you're capable of. As I sit here, watching the Italian sun dip behind the hills, I can't help but think about what lies ahead. Italy, for all its charm and challenges, has become my home in ways I hadn't imagined. I've found my tribe. But settling here doesn't mean I've finished growing. If anything, it's the opposite.

I have aspirations, both personal and professional, that still fuel me. I want to dive deeper into the language until I can confidently join the lively debates at the local café or navigate the paperwork without needing an interpreter. My English Academy has been a rewarding endeavour, but I can see opportunities to expand, to help more people connect through language the way I've been learning to connect here. There are still corners of Italy I haven't explored and experiences I haven't yet embraced. I want to visit southern Italy, learn how to ski, learn how to cook authentic Italian dishes from scratch, and maybe even write another book, one that captures the second act of my life here.

But more than anything, I think about my children. This move wasn't just for me but for them, too. I want them to see that life doesn't have to follow a rigid path, that reinvention is possible at any stage, that taking risks can lead to incredible rewards and that it's never too late to chase the life you want. If there's a legacy I hope to leave them, it's this: life is meant to be lived fully, courageously and with an open heart. Wherever the road leads next, I'm ready to follow it, not just for myself, but for the lessons I can pass on to them.

Chapter 25
Teatro Del Silenzio and the Bocelli Family Restaurant

I live 25 minutes from the Teatro del Silenzio, in the municipality of Lajatico, Andrea Bocelli's home. Every year he organises a concert there and sings in this beautiful open-air theatre in the Tuscan countryside.

This year, 2024, marks Bocelli's 30th anniversary in music, and he hosted a grand celebration concert. The concert dates were mid-July, and he had an all-star cast joining him: Ed Sheeran, Shania Twain, Sophia Carson, David Foster, Sofia Vergara, Nadine Sierra, Lang Lang, Russell Crowe, Giorgia, Lauren Daigle, Bryn Terfel, Virginia Bocelli (his daughter), Laura Pausini, Jon Batiste, José Carreras, Plácido Domingo, Tiziano Ferro, Katharine McPhee, Zucchero, Christian Nodal, Aida Garifullina, and Matteo Bocelli (his son) – and that was just a part of the list. I looked at the price of the tickets and I just couldn't justify spending that amount for one concert. Unfortunately, I was going to miss it.

I received a message one evening from one of my followers saying that she had a proposition for me. I have had a number of propositions – some bolder than others – but I asked her to fire away. She said she would buy me a ticket for the Bocelli concert if I took my followers with me, i.e. she asked me to record the experience and shared it online. I was completely flattered by this proposal but immediately turned it down. I couldn't do that. The person persisted, explaining that there was no way she could be there in person but that she desperately wanted to experience the event. Some toing and froing later, a ticket was emailed to me – it seemed I was going to the anniversary concert.

I recorded my experience before, during and after the event, capturing bits and pieces from start to finish. I showed exactly what it was like to be there. It was an incredible evening.

This was a once-in-a-lifetime event, celebrating three decades of Andrea Bocelli's musical career. The atmosphere was electric, with fans from all over the world gathering to witness this monumental occasion. I made sure to capture every moment, from the journey to the theatre to the final encore. Everyone saw the stunning landscape of Tuscany, the excitement of the crowd and, of course, the incredible performances. It was a night to remember. Whether you are a fan of Andrea Bocelli or just love good music, this concert was something special.

In addition to the concert, let me take you to a wonderful afternoon at Andrea Bocelli's restaurant, or rather, the renowned Bocelli family restaurant, *Officine Bocelli.* It is a must-stop in the heart of Tuscany, offering an experience that is both intimate and extraordinary. From the moment I walked in, I knew I was in for something special.

The ambiance of the restaurant was warm and inviting, with rustic decor that spoke of its rich heritage – wooden beams, vintage photographs, multiple farm-machinery books hanging from the ceiling. The gentle hum of conversation filled the air, creating a cosy and welcoming atmosphere. The aroma of freshly prepared food wafted through the building, making my mouth water even before I saw the menu.

I had heard so much about Officine Bocelli, famous for its traditional Italian cuisine, and it certainly did not disappoint. The highlight of my meal was the gnocchetti, small pasta dumplings that were a specialty of the house. These baby gnocchi were crafted to perfection, each bite offering a burst of flavour that was both comforting and exquisite. Cooked al dente, they had a delightful texture that paired beautifully with the rich, blue cheese sauce they were served in.

The gnocchetti was the main dish I tasted, but I started with a selection of antipasti, including bruschetta topped with ripe tomatoes, fragrant basil and a drizzle of olive oil. Each bite was a reminder of the simple yet profound joys of Italian cuisine. As I ate, I couldn't help but notice the passion and dedication that went into every aspect of the restaurant. The Bocelli family has a long history with delicious food, and their commitment to excellence was evident in every detail. From the carefully curated wine list, featuring the best local wines, to the attentive service that made me feel like an honoured guest, everything about my experience was exceptional.

One of the most memorable moments of my visit was meeting Alberto Bocelli, the younger brother of the singer Andrea, and the head of the restaurant business. He made his way through the dining room, greeting patrons and sharing stories about the restaurant's history and his family's love for food. When he reached my table, he spoke with genuine warmth and enthusiasm, eager to hear about my experience and to ensure that everything was to my liking.

For dessert, I indulged in a classic tiramisu, a heavenly concoction of coffee-soaked biscuit fingers, creamy mascarpone with a dusting of cocoa. It was the perfect ending to a perfect meal – a sweet reminder of why Italian cuisine is loved around the world.

It was clear that this was more than just a place to eat. It was a place where food, family, tradition and innovation came together to create something truly special. The warmth of the Bocelli family, the beauty of the setting and the extraordinary flavours of the food all combined to make this an unforgettable experience. If you ever find yourself in Tuscany, a visit to the Bocelli family restaurant is an absolute must. The blue cheese gnocchetti alone is worth the trip, but the entire experience – from the ambiance to the hospitality, to the exquisite cuisine, to the soft tones of brother Andrea singing in the background – is something that will stay with you long after the meal is over. As I left the restaurant, I carried with me not only the memory of a delicious meal but also the feeling of having been part of something truly special.

If there's one thing I've learned, it's that change is the only constant. In July 2023, I was a different person in a completely different setting. It's amazing how quickly life can turn around, and the transformation can be nothing short of miraculous. This time last year, I was standing in a garage in Northern Ireland buying a thin ham sandwich for lunch. The rain was pouring down, and the skies were a miserable shade of grey. I remember the feeling of dampness seeping through my coat and the cold biting at my fingers. It wasn't just the weather that was dreary; it felt like my entire existence was cloaked in a layer of dark clouds. Every day, I would take my uninspiring lunch back to an equally uninspiring office. It was a small, windowless room that seemed to sap the life out of me. The walls were a dull beige, and the fluorescent lights buzzed incessantly, casting a harsh glow on everything. There was no view to speak of, just the same four walls day in and day out.

Fast forward to today, and my life couldn't be more different. Now, I sit here in the warm embrace of the Tuscan sun, looking out at a view that takes my breath away every single day. The landscape is a vibrant tapestry of rolling hills, lush vineyards and quaint villages. The sky is a brilliant blue, and the air is filled with the scent of flowers and freshly cut grass. For lunch, I'm enjoying a bowl of sweet, juicy strawberries, bought this morning from a local market.

It's hard to believe how much has changed in this short time. From rain-soaked days to this colourful, sun-drenched paradise, the transformation is profound. It's not just the scenery that's different; my entire outlook on life has been transformed. I've learned to appreciate the little things, to find joy in the simple pleasures and to embrace every moment with gratitude. This dramatic shift in my life is a powerful reminder that we have the power to change our circumstances. It might not happen overnight, and it might require a leap of faith, but it's possible. Looking back, I realise that those dreary days were a catalyst for change. They pushed me to seek something better, to dream of a life that was rich and fulfilling. Change is inevitable, but it's also what makes life exciting. It teaches us resilience, adaptability and the importance of living in the moment. So, if you ever find yourself in a place that doesn't bring you joy, remember that you have the power to change it. Sometimes, all it takes is a little courage and a vision of a better life.

Above left: The Academy ready for children.

Above: Puccini's statute, Lucca.

Below left: A house in Peccioli.

Below: Dad having to stand on his tiptoes as they're all so tall.

Above: Ancer and Elle from Carpe Diem.

Right: Tagliatelle with porcini mushrooms from Carpe Diem.

Below: Some of the 18 chapels still remaining in San Vivaldo or the 'Jerusalem of Tuscany'.

Above: A stall at a local market.

Above right: Cake time at one of my favourite pasticcerie.

Right: The Church of San Regolo in Montaione town square, dating back to 1369.

Above: The beautiful restaurant Casa Masi, in Montaione.

Left: The Tuscan route of the famous via Francigena, a 220km section of a pilgrimage that starts at Canterbury Cathedral and ends in Rome. It passes by the town of Montaione.

Chapter 26
Tipping, Mercato Centrale and Restaurant Carpe Diem

One of the most fascinating aspects I've encountered when eating out is the Italian approach to tipping. It's a peek into the heart of Italian culture and the pride they take in their work. At the beginning of my journey here I found myself in a wonderful, cosy Italian restaurant, Il Caminetto, with the aroma of fresh pasta wafting through the air and the clinking of wine glasses creating a gentle and warming atmosphere. The server, with a warm smile, presented my meal as if it was a masterpiece. The service was impeccable, and everything was perfect. Coming from the UK or Ireland, at the end of such an evening, when paying, your natural instinct is to leave a decent tip to acknowledge and appreciate good service. I left a note on the counter as a tip, and the waiter looked at me as if I had just taken a bite of his arm. I explained that I was thanking him for fabulous service, and his face became quizzical – 'But that's what I'm here for. That's what I do. I do not need to be paid extra for giving you the service that you, as a guest, expect and deserve.' This was a revelation to me, and it made a lot of sense. These servers are professional waiters and waitresses, who are amazing at what they do, and they take great pride in doing it. I now understand the questioning head-tilt when he saw me leaving extra money for good service.

I'm not saying they wouldn't appreciate a tip or that they don't tip in other parts of Italy. It is just an interesting variation on the theme of tipping that I have experienced here in rural Tuscany. It's a cultural nuance that took me by surprise. The attitude here is that the server gives wonderful service because it's their job, not because they expect something extra. It is unusual, especially coming from a culture where tipping is almost second nature. To rural Italians, tipping implies that they've gone above and beyond, but in their minds, they've just done what they always do – give wonderful service.

Living in Italy is an endless journey of exploration and discovery, where even the simplest outing can turn into a memorable adventure. One such experience that stands out vividly in my mind is a visit to the Mercato Centrale in Florence, a place that captures the essence of Italian culture in its most vibrant form. I headed there one Tuesday morning, hoping to beat the crowds – ha. The Mercato Centrale (Central Market) is a must-visit for anyone visiting Florence. As I approached, the bustling energy of the place was palpable. The market was alive with activity, packed full of people from all walks of life, each absorbed in their own little slice of this bustling centre.

The first thing that struck me upon entering was the sheer variety of offerings. This wasn't just a place to buy food; it was a feast for the senses. The vibrant colours of fresh fruits and vegetables were laid out in a dazzling array, each stall competing for attention. The aroma of fresh produce mingled with the rich, savoury scents of meats and cheeses, creating an intoxicating blend that made your mouth water. It's not just about buying ingredients; it's about experiencing the food culture in its most authentic form. As I wandered through the market, I found myself drawn to a stall selling fresh seafood. The display was immaculate, with fish, shrimp and other delicacies arranged in neat, glistening rows. The fishmonger, with a friendly smile, expertly filleted a fish for a customer, his hands moving with the practised ease of someone who has spent a lifetime perfecting his craft.

Moving on, I found myself in the section dedicated to meats and cold cuts. Here, the stalls were laden with an impressive selection of cured meats, sausages and hams. The rich, smoky aroma of prosciutto mingled with the spicy scent of salami, creating a mouth-watering experience. Shoppers moved from stall to stall, sampling slices of meat offered by vendors eager to share.

The market isn't just about traditional Italian fare, though. It's also a melting pot of culinary influences from around the world. I passed by stalls offering Chinese food, sushi and curry, evidence of the diverse foodie landscape of modern Italy. The upper level of the market is home to a variety of restaurants and bars, where people can sit and enjoy a meal and a drink. Here, the atmosphere is more relaxed, with diners chatting over plates of food and glasses of wine, savouring the flavours and the moment. The building itself is a work of art, with its high ceilings and intricate ironwork. The natural light streaming in from above bathed the market in a warm, inviting glow, highlighting the colours and textures of the hall below. It's a place that feels alive, not just with the hustle of commerce but also with the history and culture of Florence itself.

As I continued to explore, I couldn't help but be drawn to the sweet treats on offer. The *dolce*, or sweets, section of the market is a paradise for anyone with a sweet tooth. Here, you can find everything from traditional Italian pastries to gelato, each one more tempting than the last. I watched as a vendor expertly scooped out servings of rich, creamy gelato – the cool, smooth texture a perfect counterpoint to the warm day. The market has transformed from a place where people come to buy food to a destination where they can enjoy upmarket street food. This isn't your typical street food; it's a step above, offering a variety of high-quality dishes that cater to all tastes. From fresh seafood, pasta and meats to sushi and Chinese food, there's something for everyone.

After spending a few hours exploring, tasting and taking in the sights and sounds, it was time to head home. I made my way towards the train station. As I walked, the sun began to set, casting a golden glow over the city. The streets of Florence, with their historic charm and lively atmosphere, felt even more magical in the evening light. The visit to the Mercato Centrale was a chance to connect with the city's vibrant culture and its people. It's experiences like these that make living in Italy so special. The Mercato Centrale is a place that stays with you long after you've left, its sights, sounds and flavours lingering in your memory.

Another experience I want to share is one I had at a new

restaurant that has just opened its doors in my hometown. The restaurant, Carpe Diem, promised not only delicious food but also a stunning panoramic view that simply had to be seen to be believed. The story of Carpe Diem began a few months ago when I posted about a beloved local restaurant that had closed after its owners decided to retire. This restaurant, previously known as Panorama, was cherished for its breathtaking views and delicious cuisine. Naturally, when I heard that new owners, the lovely Ancer and Elle, had taken over and were reopening the venue under the name Carpe Diem. I was curious and keen to try it out.

The day of the grand opening arrived, and I was thrilled to be invited to the inaugural event. The name Carpe Diem, Latin for Seize the Day, seemed apt as I was ready to make the most of this experience. From the moment I stepped inside, it was clear that the new owners had put their heart and soul into revamping the place. The restaurant was beautifully decorated, blending modern elegance with rustic charm. Large windows lined the walls, offering diners an unobstructed view of the surrounding landscape. The panoramic vista was nothing short of spectacular. The rolling hills, dotted with cypress trees, stretched out as far as the eye could see, creating a serene and enchanting backdrop.

I was joined by some of my closest Italian friends, a wonderful family who have embraced me since I arrived in Italy. We were all excited to see what Carpe Diem had to offer. As we settled into our seats, the atmosphere was filled with a sense of anticipation and joy. The restaurant was buzzing with guests, all eager to try the menu and take in the views.

The menu at Carpe Diem was a delightful mix of traditional Italian dishes with a modern twist. Each item was crafted with care, highlighting the freshness and quality of local ingredients. Our meal began with a selection of antipasti that set the tone for the evening. We savoured bruschetta topped with juicy tomatoes and fragrant basil, thin slices of prosciutto wrapped around sweet melon and a variety of cheeses that melted in our mouths. For my main dish, I chose a classic Tuscan dish, *Bistecca alla Fiorentina*, a thick, juicy steak cooked to perfection. The meat was tender and flavourful, seasoned simply with olive oil, salt and pepper, allowing the quality of the beef to shine through. My friends opted for a variety of dishes, from rich, creamy risottos to fresh, handmade pasta with succulent seafood. Each dish was beautifully presented, a feast for the eyes as well as the palate.

Throughout the meal, we shared stories, laughter and, of course, plenty of wine. My friends, ever the patient and encouraging bunch, insisted that I practise my Italian. Despite my protests about having a *molto vecchio* (very old) head, they were determined to help me improve. Our conversations were a mix of stuttered English and stuttered Italian, filled with heartfelt encouragement.

As we enjoyed our meal, the sun began to set, casting a glow over the landscape. The view from Carpe Diem lived up to its reputation, and then some. The setting sun painted the sky in oranges, pinks and purples, creating a breathtaking outlook that complemented the delicious food and wonderful company. It was one of those moments where everything felt perfect, a snapshot of pure contentment.

For dessert, we indulged in some traditional Italian sweets. Tiramisu was a crowd favourite. We also sampled panna cotta, a silky-smooth dessert served with a tart berry compote, and cannoli filled with sweet ricotta cheese. Each dessert was a delicious fitting end to a meal that had been a true celebration of Italian cuisine. Carpe Diem had exceeded all expectations, not just with its food, but with its ambiance and the sense of community it fostered. The new owners have done an incredible job of preserving the spirit of the old Panorama while infusing it with their own unique touch. It was clear that Carpe Diem was destined to become a favourite among locals and visitors. It had provided us not only with a memorable dining experience but also with a beautiful evening of friendship and connection. It was a reminder of the simple joys in life – good food, great company and the beauty of the world around us. As I continue my journey through Italy, I look forward to many more experiences like this one, moments of connection, discovery and joy that make life truly special.

Throughout our life, we often come across words and phrases that resonate deeply within us. Recently, I stumbled upon a quote that struck me profoundly: 'You have two lives, and the second one begins when you realise you only have one.' (Confucius). This simple yet powerful statement encapsulates a universal truth about the human experience, one that is both humbling and enlightening.

The essence of this quote lies in its recognition of growth and maturity as pivotal moments in our lives. Initially, we live our lives almost in autopilot, driven by routines, societal expectations and a sense of invincibility that often accompanies youth. We go through the motions, making no plans, mostly taking everything for granted. This is our first life, a period marked by exploration, learning and, often, a certain naïveté about the finite nature of our lives. As we grow older and gain life experience, a shift occurs. We begin to understand the true value of time and the fleeting nature of our days. This realisation marks the beginning of our second life. It's a moment of awakening, where we come to terms with our mortality and the fact that we have only one life to live. This awareness brings with it a profound change in perspective, guiding us to live more intentionally and meaningfully.

In this second life, we start to prioritise what truly matters. We focus more on our passions, relationships and the things that bring us genuine joy and fulfilment. We become more mindful of how we spend our time and with whom we spend it. The mundane and trivial concerns that once occupied our thoughts begin to fade, making way for deeper reflections. This newfound awareness also brings a sense of urgency. Knowing that our time is limited can be a powerful motivator to chase our dreams, mend broken relationships, end abusive relationships and pursue a life that aligns with our values and aspirations. It encourages us to take risks, embrace opportunities and live with fewer regrets. This isn't to say that we should live recklessly, but rather that we should live with a conscious appreciation for the present moment.

Moreover, this realisation helps us to cultivate a sense of gratitude. We become more thankful for simple pleasures – a beautiful sunset, a heartfelt conversation, the laughter of loved ones. These moments, which we might have previously overlooked, take on a new significance, enriching our lives in ways we never imagined. Gratitude, in turn, brings about a greater sense of contentment and peace.

The concept of having two lives also highlights the importance of continuous growth and self-discovery. Just because we reach this point of realisation doesn't mean our journey of growth ends. On the contrary, it becomes even more crucial. We continue to learn, evolve and adapt, finding new ways to enhance our lives and the lives of those around us. This perpetual growth is what keeps us engaged and passionate, fuelling our desire to make the most of our one precious life.

As I continue in Italy, this quote has taken on a special meaning for me. Living in a place that is steeped in history and beauty has reinforced the idea that life is a series of moments, each one precious and fleeting. The experiences I've had, the people I've met and the places I've seen have all contributed to my understanding of what it means to truly live. So, as I continue to explore and experience the beauty of Italy, I carry this wisdom with me. It guides my actions, shapes my decisions and enriches my life here. And as I share these reflections with you, I hope they inspire you to embrace your own second life, to live fully and authentically, and to appreciate the incredible gift of existence.

Chapter 27
Slowly Changing Perspectives

Learning Italian at my age has been problematic, to say the least. The language is beautiful, but it has a way of tangling itself around your tongue and tying you in knots. I've made some memorable mistakes, each more mortifying than the last. I'm walking about like a toddler trying to understand what is happening – not the most comfortable place to be when you're approaching your mid-fifties. I've already mentioned my loud and confident request for a 'bicycle of Chianti' rather than a 'glass of Chianti' in a bar full of listening Italians.

Then there's the Italian concept of *domani*. It means 'tomorrow', but I've come to learn that it's more of a hopeful wispy suggestion than a promise or a date fixed in a calendar. Early on, I waited eagerly for a repairman who assured me he'd come *domani*. He didn't show up until a week later, breezing in with a smile and a shrug. Bite your lip, Barry, and smile back. What these moments taught me, though, was to let go of perfection. Life here isn't about getting everything right. It's about showing up, trying and laughing when things don't go as planned. And honestly, it makes life much more interesting and so much less stressful.

Moving to a new country can feel like walking into a party where you don't know a soul and can't understand the language. Italians have a way of helping you out, offering gestures of kindness that make a stranger feel at home. One of my first encounters with this warmth came shortly after I started decorating the English Academy. My neighbour, an elderly gentleman, knocked on my door holding out his hand for a shake saying, '*Benvenuto*' (Welcome).

The Italians here have their work–life balance down to an artform. They master it effortlessly. Work exists, of course, and they work hard, but it's never allowed to overshadow life itself. Lunch isn't just a meal; it's a ritual. Shops close for hours in the afternoon so people can go home, eat with their families and perhaps take a nap. It's a rhythm I've come to admire deeply. I remember this same elderly neighbour walking passed my English school heading for lunch. He popped his head in and said, *'Barry, lavorare per vivere, non vivere per lavorare'* (Barry, work to live, don't live to work). It's a simple sentiment, but true.

And then there's the Italian life lessons that sneak up on you in the most casual ways. There's Matteo, who runs the flower stall at the market. He has a way of handing you a flower and, in the same breath, saying, 'In Italy, Barry, we eat slow, talk fast and never forget dessert. It's good for the heart.' Or the local café owner, who once stopped mid-espresso pour to tell me, 'You're learning Italian too seriously. Relax. The words will come when you stop chasing them.' These moments aren't grand gestures, but they've shaped me in ways I didn't expect. Italians have a knack of showing you what really matters – family, friends, good food and taking time to savour it all. Their lessons are never delivered with lectures, only with smiles, a pat on the back or, sometimes, a couple of additional plants in my shopping box. What I've learned from these people is that life isn't about rushing to the finish line. It's about enjoying the adventure, one shared meal, one conversation, one gift at a time.

One of the first things I noticed about living in Italy was how different time felt here. It wasn't just the clocks ticking the same seconds, but the way people moved, how they spoke and even how they paused in between tasks. In Northern Ireland, time had always felt like something I was chasing. In Italy, time was something to live with, not against. Take mornings, for instance. Pre-Italy, I would gulp down a cup of coffee, half-listen to the radio and rush out the door. Here, mornings are a ritual. A small espresso, sipped slowly at the café counter, becomes a moment to greet familiar faces, exchange pleasantries and simply be. There's no takeaway cup in sight, just porcelain cups and people leaning into the moment.

This shift isn't just about mornings. The entire day operates on a slower rhythm. Shops close in the middle of the afternoon and no one bats an eyelid. It's understood that this is time for lunch, family, maybe a wee vino and a rest. At first, it baffled me. Where has everyone gone? But as I adjusted, I realised this slower pace feels more human – it's just so much more civilised. I started finding joy in the simplicity of it all. Tending to the flowers on my terrace, a task I would have brushed off as unproductive in my former life, has become a source of calm. Watching the buds slowly bloom and the colours shift through the seasons has taught me to appreciate the beauty of patience.

Even errands feel less like chores and more like mini adventures. A trip to the market isn't about ticking items off a list, but about wandering through the stalls, greeting vendors and letting my senses guide me – choosing peaches because they smell perfect or oranges because they are massive and have caught my eye. I often just sit with a gelato in hand watching the world go by. Taking a moment to sit on a bench, spoon in hand, while the sun warms my face is pure luxury – even on an ordinary Tuesday.

The contrast to my old life couldn't be starker. In Northern Ireland, there was always something to do, somewhere to be. Days felt like a race to a finish line that was never quite reached. I often measured success in terms of productivity – how much I'd achieved, how much I'd planned for the next day. Instead, here, I've learned to measure success in terms of satisfaction. Did I enjoy today? Did I notice something beautiful? Did I laugh? This isn't to say I've completely abandoned the sense of urgency I used to live with. It still bubbles up occasionally, but I'm learning to let go of the rush. If the train's late, it's late. If dinner takes an extra 20 minutes to be delivered in a restaurant, then that's 20 minutes to sip wine and enjoy the occasion. Time in Italy isn't a thing to conquer. It's something to flow with, to embrace, to savour. And in learning to live this way, I've discovered a kind of freedom I never knew I needed.

Exploring the markets here is a kind of culinary education. The vendors are patient with my halting Italian, offering samples of cheeses, cured meats and fruits I've never tasted before. Once, at the height of the Christmas season, I found myself captivated by an entire aisle of panettone, the iconic Italian sweet bread. I bought one on impulse. These can be the size of a small suitcase. It took me weeks to finish it, but every bite reminded me of the season's warmth and abundance. Food has also become my bridge to the community. I'll never forget my first truffle festival in San Miniato. The air was thick with the intoxicating aroma of white truffles, and tables were piled high with delicacies. I joined a group of locals for lunch, and we feasted on *tagliolini al tartufo* – a dish so rich and earthy that I felt as if I were eating the forest itself. As we ate, stories flowed freely, laughter filled the air and, for the first time, I felt as if I belonged. Sharing meals has a way of breaking down barriers. Whether it's a casual dinner with neighbours or a feast at a festival, food creates a space where differences fade and connections deepen.

If there's one thing Italy has taught me, it's the power of saying yes to new experiences, to unfamiliar challenges and to moments that seem insignificant at first but turn out to shape you in unexpected ways. My initiation into this mindset came in the form of a game I'd never heard of – padel. I was walking past a local sports centre one day when I saw a group of people playing on what looked like a mini tennis court enclosed by glass walls. I stopped to watch. After a while, one of the players called out '*Vuoi provare?*' (Want to try?). Absolutely! The next day I was at my first padel lesson. Padel, as I learned, is a mix of tennis and squash, played with smaller racquets and a slower-moving ball. It looks simple enough until you're actually on the court, flailing around. My instructor, Gianmarco, was patient to a fault: 'Barry, you're doing great. Keep it up.' By the end of the session, I was sweating and sore, but had enjoyed every minute. That one impulsive 'yes' led to a routine. I started attending weekly padel games, slowly improving and, more importantly, forming friendships. The sport became less about winning and more about the camaraderie – the high-fives after a good shot, the teasing over missed ones and the post-game espresso where we'd sit around and talk about everything and nothing.

Each of these moments, small as they seemed at the time, taught me something profound. They showed me that growth doesn't come from staying in your comfort zone; it comes from stepping out, even if you stumble along the way. To anyone reading this, my message is simple – say yes. Say yes to the awkward, the challenging, the new. You don't have to be perfect at it, and you don't have to love it forever. But you might surprise yourself. You might discover a new hobby, meet people who change your perspective or simply gather stories to laugh about later. Italy hasn't been just a location for me, but a series of invitations to live more fully. And every time I've said yes, it's rewarded me with something I didn't even know I needed.

Chapter 28
Typical Tuscan Dishes

I always knew the food in Italy would be good, and when I used to come here as a tourist it was. However, I was usually coming as a dad of three young children, so I didn't necessarily seek out restaurants making typical Tuscan dishes or focus too much on dishes beyond plain(ish). Being here now, though – wow, bring it on! I have found the food here to be beyond outstanding. It has opened a whole new world to me where fresh food is at the centre.

I have been here for just over a year now, and I genuinely haven't had one bad meal. I usually eat out maybe three times a week, either lunch or dinner, and I pay half the price I would pay in the UK or Ireland – and that would include a glass or two of local wine.

I've approached some of my favourite restaurants in this area and have asked the head chefs to reproduce some of my favourite typical Tuscan dishes. If you're ever in this area, please try these dishes made by the chefs themselves – if not, have a go at making them yourself. The restaurants I visit often and have chosen include Carpe Diem, Casa Masi, l'Ciampa and Daniela, my principal in 'Cooking with Nonna'.

Carpe Diem

At the heart of Ristorante Carpe Diem is the inspiring story of Ancer Flores and Eleonora Gonnelli, a couple whose passion for hospitality and cuisine transcends borders. Ancer, originally from Guatemala, and Eleonora, born in the charming Tuscan town of Poggibonsi, united their diverse cultures and shared dream to create a place where food and hospitality come alive.

They write:

Opening our own restaurant was far from easy. The road was filled with challenges, sacrifices and countless late nights, but our unwavering determination and love for our craft kept us moving forward. For us, Ristorante Carpe Diem is more than a business; it's a labour of love and a dream come true.

We pour our hearts into making every guest's visit a unique and memorable experience. With a deep commitment to quality and detail, we create an atmosphere that feels both warm and special. We believe in the power of simplicity, authenticity and a genuine smile to make people feel at home.

Located in the heart of Montaione, Restaurant Carpe Diem is a haven for those seeking an unforgettable culinary experience. Combining timeless elegance with a warm and inviting atmosphere, it sets the stage for intimate dinners, celebratory gatherings and cherished moments. The cuisine, inspired by the rich heritage of Tuscan tradition, showcases an artful balance of authenticity and creativity. Every dish is meticulously prepared using fresh, high-quality ingredients, ensuring that every bite is a celebration of flavour.

The menu is a journey through Tuscany's gastronomic treasures, offering seasonal delicacies and innovative culinary creations that delight even the most discerning palates. To elevate the dining experience, Carpe Diem boasts a carefully curated selection of wines from Italy's most renowned vineyards, perfectly paired to complement each dish. With attentive and personalised service that anticipates every need, Restaurant Carpe Diem doesn't just serve meals but also crafts memories. It's more than a restaurant; it's a destination where every guest leaves with a story to tell and a longing to return.

Tagliatelle with porcini mushrooms

Ingredients for the pasta:
340g all-purpose flour (00)
80g semolina flour
Pinch of salt
4 whole eggs
2 egg yolks
1 teaspoon extra virgin olive oil

Ingredients for the sauce:
500ml vegetable broth
10g dried porcini mushrooms
600g fresh porcini mushrooms
4 tablespoons extra virgin olive oil
1 glove garlic
1 shallot
120ml white wine
Salt to taste
1 small bunch parsley
1 chilli pepper (optional, to taste)

Method:
When you're ready to make tagliatelle with porcini mushrooms, start with the pasta. On a work surface, mix the two types of flour, add a pinch of salt and form a crater in the centre. Place the lightly beaten eggs and yolks in the middle, then add about 1 teaspoon of olive oil.

Begin mixing the eggs with the flour, working from the centre outward, using a fork initially, then continue by hand. Once the mixture starts to come together, knead it by hand until you have a smooth and homogeneous dough. Wrap the dough in plastic wrap and refrigerate for 30 minutes. Meanwhile, enrich the vegetable broth by adding the dried porcini mushrooms. Keep it warm over a low heat. While waiting, remove any dirt from the fresh mushrooms and clean them with a damp cloth.

Remove the dough from the fridge, and roll it out to a thickness of about 1 mm, using a small amount of flour if needed. If using a pasta machine, roll it to setting '5'. Alternatively, use a rolling pin. Cut the dough into rectangles about 25–30 cm long, then slice them into strips slightly narrower than 1 cm to form the tagliatelle.

Slice the mushroom stems thinly and heat a drizzle of olive oil in a pan. Add the peeled garlic clove and thinly sliced shallot. When the mixture starts sizzling, add the prepared mushroom stems. Add a little broth and cook over low heat for 3–4 minutes. Increase the heat, deglaze with white wine, remove the garlic and add the mushroom caps sliced into thin pieces. Season with salt, add a little more broth and cook for another 3–4 minutes, keeping the mixture moist by adding hot broth as needed.

Boil the tagliatelle in salted boiling water for 2–3 minutes, then drain and transfer them to the pan with the sauce. Stir and let them absorb the flavour for a few moments, adding a little more of the hot broth to loosen the sauce. Garnish with chopped parsley and serve. If desired, add thinly sliced chilli peppers to individual servings. Enjoy your delicious tagliatelle with porcini mushrooms!

Casa Masi

Casa Masi is a beautiful restaurant on the outskirts of Montaione situated within a restored centuries-old farmhouse. Meals can be taken indoors or, on finer evenings, in a stunning garden setting.

They write:

> Since the day Casa Masi opened, we have preserved the old wisdom of culinary Tuscan traditions. Far from

'industrially assembled' kitchens, we focus primarily on produce from our rich land while paying full respect to food that is in season. In our cooking, we avoid the 'culinary pollution' by using only raw ingredients that are cooked strictly following old recipes – for example, using goat cottage cheese (once the only type of milk children could drink) and chickpea flour for making handmade tagliatelle, which we sometimes swap for chestnut flour in winter. We are continuing the gastronomic traditions of the region by preserving knowledge of the specific plants of our land and recovering the wisdom of our grandmothers and their recipe books for syrups, marmalades, aromatic plants and special courses – in essence, we are tightly weaving together stories of yesterday to those of today.

Pecorino gnocchi with pear sauce
(serves 4)

Ingredients:
300g ricotta
1 whole egg
200g Tuscan-seasoned pecorino cheese
Salt and pepper to taste
Flour as needed
3 pears
50g butter
Cinnamon

Method:
In a bowl, work the ricotta well with the egg and grated pecorino (we refer to well-seasoned Tuscan pecorino cheese, which is tender and soft). Add salt and pepper to taste and let it thicken slowly with flour, avoiding lumps. Make small and slightly flattened balls from this

dough.

In the meantime, prepare the sauce: peel the pears (which should be very ripe and juicy), and cut them into cubes. Cook them in lots of salted boiling water. Take them from the water when they rise to the top.

Meanwhile melt the butter in a small frying pan, flavour with cinnamon, add the pears and cook them over a slow flame for 5 minutes.

Gently immerse the gnocchi in the pear sauce and serve immediately. This is a dish in which sweet and sour are perfectly amalgamated.

l'Ciampa

l'Ciampa is a lovely family-run restaurant in the heart of Montaione. The restaurant sits within the walls of the town overlooking the Tuscan countryside. It is owned by two brothers, and family members are also involved in producing their delicious food. I have found the waiting staff in l'Ciampa to be the friendliest I have come across. They are always smiling and nothing is too much trouble for them.

Wild Boar Stew

(serves 5)

Ingredients:
1.5kg selected wild boar meat
1l red wine
2 onions
2 carrots
2 celery stalks
Extra virgin olive oil
Spices (bay leaves, cinnamon, cloves, etc.)
500g peeled tomatoes
Salt and pepper to taste

Method:

The evening before cooking, cut the wild boar meat into fairly large cubes. Place it in a large bowl and cover it with half the wine and the same amount of water – it's important that the meat is completely submerged. Roughly chop half of the vegetables (the 'aromatics') and add them to the bowl. Leave to marinate overnight in a cool place.

The next day, drain the wild boar meat and discard the aromatics. Then place the meat in a large pan and cook slowly over low heat until it releases its juices.

Drain everything through a colander. Meanwhile, finely chop the remaining vegetables and sauté them in the same pan with a generous amount of extra virgin olive oil.

Add the wild boar meat back into the pan, sear it briefly and then deglaze with the remaining red wine.

Add the spices, peeled tomatoes, salt and pepper. Stir occasionally and cook until tender, adding a ladleful of water now and then if needed.

Serve decorated with a few bay leaves, and if you like, some black olives. It's delicious served with sautéed spinach, roast potatoes or fried artichokes – and accompanied by Tuscan bread. Enjoy!

Daniela – My Italian 'Cooking with Nonna'

Daniela arrived at my office during my first weeks as an English teacher. Over the following months we became friends as I taught her and her adult daughter English. Daniela and her family invited me to their property many times to enjoy their hospitality and Daniela's amazing cooking. During one of these meals, I asked Daniela to show some of my guests how she prepares and cooks typical Italian dishes, and she agreed to be the principal in my 'Cooking with Nonna' weeks. Nonna is Italian for grandmother.

Daniela writes:

I come from a family of restaurateurs. When I was young, I worked for a few years in a restaurant with my parents. My first post was in the kitchen, where I worked alongside a chef who was quite protective of his work, but with a young and inexperienced girl like me, he let his guard down a bit and taught me the basic preparations. I whipped cream for hours on end, made mayonnaise by hand endlessly, prepared crepe shells until exhaustion – but in doing so, I had the chance to watch and learn with my eyes what was not explained to me in words.

My mother was an excellent cook when it came to traditional Tuscan cuisine, so after some time, we decided to run the kitchen together. She didn't know anything about cooking fish, but in the meantime, I had learned, and so we divided the tasks between us. With her, I was also able to learn more about traditional cooking.

After a few years, I began my professional career linked to the studies I had pursued. I got married and, little by little, I left the restaurant. However, my passion for cooking always remained, and, fortunately, I managed to pass it on to my daughters, who today are even better in the kitchen than I am. This feels like an invisible thread that continues to connect us through the generations, and it makes me happy and proud.

Stewed baby octopus (*Moscardini in Umido*)

Ingredients:
1 carrot
1 celery stalk
½ onion
1 clove garlic
1 chilli pepper
Olive oil
1kg baby octopus
100ml white wine
300g tomato purée
Salt
300ml vegetable broth
Slices of bread

Method:
Clean and finely chop the carrot, celery, onion, garlic and chilli pepper. Place the chopped vegetables in a pan with olive oil and cook over a medium heat for 5 minutes, allowing them to soften and slightly colour. Add the cleaned and washed baby octopus, let them cook for 5 minutes to absorb the flavours. Pour in the white wine and raise the heat for 1 minute to allow the alcohol to evaporate.

Lower the heat, add the tomato purée, season with salt and cook covered, over a low heat, for about 50 minutes, adding vegetable broth little by little as needed to keep the sauce soft. Uncover and increase the heat slightly to reduce the sauce to your desired consistency.

Toast thin slices of bread, arrange them on a serving tray, pour the sauce and baby octopus over them. Serve hot.

Chicken roll (*Rotolo di Pollo*)

Ingredients:

1kg chicken breast
100g minced veal
1 pork sausage
1 egg
Parsley
3 slices cooked ham
3 slices scamorza cheese
1 tablespoon finely chopped rosemary, sage and garlic
Salt and pepper
1 tablespoon flour
100ml red wine
150ml milk
150ml vegetable broth

Method:

Open the chicken breast, debone it, and spread it out into a single flat piece without any holes. Mix the minced veal with the sausage and spread a thin layer over the chicken.

Prepare a thin omelette with the egg and parsley, place it over the meat mixture, and then add the ham and cheese on top.

Roll up the chicken breast tightly and tie it with kitchen twine to keep the filling inside during cooking. Rub the rolled-up chicken with the chopped herbs and lightly flour it. Place it in a pan with olive oil and brown it on all sides. Add the red wine and raise the heat to evaporate the alcohol.

Lower the heat, add the milk and vegetable broth, cover and cook for 30 minutes. Remove from the heat, let it rest for 15 minutes, slice, cover with the cooking sauce and serve.

The food here is outstanding, varied, delicious and reasonably priced – way and above anything I've tasted in any other European country. If you don't get the opportunity to travel to this part of the world, please attempt to cook any/all of the above dishes. Follow the recipes provided and you will not be disappointed.

Chapter 29
The Montaionese

The Montaionese are quite simply the people of Montaione, the town in Italy where I have chosen to set up home. I have owned a place here for nine years and was initially using it as a holiday home with my family until I made the permanent move. Being here as a tourist in July is very different from being here 365.

One obvious difference you notice is the very distinct change in the weather. From October to December, the temperatures drop significantly. During December to February, it will be touching single digit degrees during the day. This is not a major change in winter temperatures from what I was experiencing in the Northern Ireland, but here, so far, the cold days also greet you with sunshine and blue skies – mostly.

The reverse is true when you hit April and May, when the temperatures rise significantly. And you'll be enjoying 30 degrees during June, July, August and September. In recent years, temperatures have been pushing 35 plus, usually in August, but it's not an uncomfortable heat here. We sit just shy of 400 metres above sea level, which gives us a cool air breeze – lovely during the warm summers. The people of the closest larger town, Castelfiorentino, which sits 50 metres above sea level, often come to Montaione during the summer for cooler evening strolls or to visit our restaurants, as the temperature is lower.

Gone are the incessant weeks of rain and seemingly eternal bleak skies that I was experiencing in Northern Ireland, and that was not just in the winter months – that could be mid-July. Of course, I can get a day here where it feels as if the world is coming to an end because it is so stormy, but then the next day the glorious sunshine returns. It obviously does rain here. You only have to look at the landscape and see 100 versions of green to know the environment isn't a stranger to rain, but in Tuscany the rain comes in bursts and not lengthy visits.

There are road signs throughout my area showing that each vehicle must carry snow chains onboard between the 1st of December and the 15th of April. I have asked the locals about this, and they say it hasn't snowed in Montaione for decades never mind any requirement for the use of snow chains. However, it is mandatory that each vehicle carries them, so I have them in Albert (my latest car).

One of the issues I was reasonably nervous about prior to moving here was how the locals would take to an outsider, especially one who couldn't speak a word of Italian. I was always of the opinion that I wanted to immerse myself in Italian life, learn the language and not be a Brit Abroad. I also didn't want to be surrounded by an ex-pat community. Immersing myself, without a word of Italian, has been the hardest exercise to date and remains so. I have a massive advantage, though, in that I am running a business, the Toscana English Academy, in the centre of the town, opposite the church. I can't escape the immersion factor, as it is necessary for everyday living.

I find that when people communicate with me, they all want to speak English – whether it is because they are students in my class, they just want to practise their English, or they are simply being polite. Initially, I always responded in English, but now I have taken the conscious decision that, to progress my Italian, I must reply to them in Italian. So, the Montaionese speak to me in pidgin English, and I respond in terrible Italian. It makes me smile, but we get there eventually. I have had a couple of Italian friends say to me, 'Barry, Barry, please speak English because we don't have a notion what you are saying when you speak in Italian.' I also had a guest ask one of the locals, 'Is Barry's Italian good?' The local replied laughing, 'He is enthusiastic.' … Oh dear.

Without exception or contradiction, I have found the people of Montaione to be wonderful. They are kind, patient, interested, interesting, humorous, genuine and charismatic. They have accepted me into their lives without question. They don't treat me as an outsider; they smile warmly and greet me as if I'd been born in the centre of the town.

They generally greet each other with '*Ciao, come stai?*' (Hello, how are you?). The response I overhear constantly is '*Bene, bene.*' (Fine, fine). When I am greeted with '*Ciao, come stai?*' I always reply '*Favoloso, grazie.*' (Fabulous, thank you). This makes them smile, and I'm not joking – to date, being here has been fabulous. Being accepted by a warm community does make you feel as if you're part of a larger team, and this makes the challenge of everyday immersion one hundred times easier.

Let me introduce you to a number of characters I have come across since moving here (first names only). There are over 3,500 people who live within Montaione, and the following few are the individuals I have come across who have gone out of their way to make my life easier and more colourful since moving here. First and foremost, there is Francesco, friend, entertainer, driver, fixer. I was painting my office during the first week when I arrived, and there was a knock on the window. I waved in a stranger, and he said, 'Hello, my name is Francesco. You can call me Frank. Welcome. I have lived in Montaione most of my life, and if you need anything at all, please ask me and I will help you.' What a wonderful thing to do and say. We have been close friends ever since. He was correct – anytime I need anything, he is there. He is one of the loveliest people I have ever met. And he can sing like Frank Sinatra, too.

Daniela and Francesca, mother and daughter, started off as strangers and students. But our relationship quickly changed to being good friends. After a few weeks of being my student, Daniela invited me to visit her family for Sunday dinner, and I was welcomed as a long-lost family member by her husband, Stefano, and their wonderful family. Daniela is a native of Montaione, and if ever I need anything, she knows the person I have to talk to. They have invited me numerous times to their home and local restaurants, and every time we laugh and enjoy the simple delights of good company. They are an amazing and loving family.

Giacomo is a lovely man. He is the local Italian lawyer. He knocked on my door one day, as he wanted to improve his English. At that stage his English wasn't great – but still better than my Italian. So, we worked together for many sessions, and his English improved significantly – so much so that he later gave me a lecture on Italian history, all in English, for one hour without a pause. Giacomo has a fabulous sense of humour, and it was with him that I first recognised that the Italian sense of humour is very much like the Irish one – quick and pointed. He is hilarious and can see humour in most conversations. He is an exceptionally clever student and is very knowledgeable on a wide range of subjects. He will often ask me to focus the lesson on, for example, Irish history or English literature.

I have also been invited to the home of another student, Clizia, and her family. The family could not have been kinder. Knowing that I was on my own at the very beginning, they asked me to join them for a delicious Sunday lunch. I have been to their home a couple of times, having been invited to a barbecue and a pizza night. Every time I felt at home and very welcome.

Clizia's uncle Emanuele is another character I have come to know. He is the Tuscan Cowboy in that he owns and runs a fabulous American-style ranch, Il Gelsomino, 300 metres from my home. He is an artist when it comes to riding horses, and he competes throughout Italy. It is with Emanuele that I take my guests to horse-ride through the vineyards. He always has a large smile on his face and is a pleasure to be around.

I also have a number of individuals that I see often, particularly the parents of the young children that I teach basic English to. I find they also have a great sense of humour. I ask the parents to stay when I teach their 4-year-old children, and I've started bringing them, the parents, into the songs that I sing. The looks, laughter and raised eyebrows tell a story, but it only encourages me to push on. The parents have presented me with gifts to thank me for taking the time with their children and, honestly, it is a pleasure, especially when I hear them progress and they can sing the likes of 'Head, Shoulders, Knees and Toes' on their own without me singing it with them. Whenever I ask the children to name an animal that is in a picture, in English, and they don't know it, then I will say it and they will repeat it. When they get it right, I will say '*Yaaaay, applauso*' and everyone will applaud. I mis-pronounced a word in Italian this week, and the children couldn't understand what I meant, so one of the parents said it correctly. I then repeated it, and the parents simultaneously shouted 'Yaaaay, applause'. Oh, I took a fit of laughing. I mostly feel like a toddler trying to communicate in Italian, but I'll get there.

Another friend is Roberto, who has shown the patience of a saint when pushing ahead and trying to talk with me in Italian (very slowly). He knocked on my office door one evening and gifted me with a litre of his homemade top-quality olive oil – delicious!

I couldn't mention local characters without writing about Matello and Simonita. Both design, make and sell leather goods, mainly handbags, on the main street in Montaione. Matello is also a skilful landscape and portrait painter. I see them every morning walking to work at 10 am, walking passed again at 12.45 pm for lunch, passing again at 4 pm as they head back to work, and again at 7.45 pm as they head home. Every day, six days a week. You may think there's nothing strange about that – until you know that Matello is 90 years old, and his wife, Simonita, is slightly younger. They are a lovely couple, and they like to stop by and chat to me about my school and the colourful flowers I have planted outside my shop. Their dedication is inspiring and a testament to their incredible work ethic and wonderful character.

The local Comune or Council is headed by a mayor. Here in Montaione, Paolo is the mayor and has been for nearly 10 years. In Tuscany, the duties and responsibilities of a mayor vary considerably from those I associate with mayors in the UK and Ireland, where the mayor takes on more of a ceremonial role. Paolo is a popular leader and is voted in during every election with a landslide of a percentage. He is ably assisted by individuals I know, Sandro, Luca and Giorgio – the latter two being my students at the Toscana English Academy. I have found the Comune to be efficient, transparent and proactive. The people in the Comune are approachable, open to suggestions and are seen out and about in the heart of the community on a daily basis. My business was open only a matter of a few weeks when I received a personal letter from the mayor, welcoming me to the community and asking if there was anything he or the community could do to assist with my transition into Italian life. I was genuinely touched by this, and it gave me some idea how I would be warmly welcomed by the entire community, and it has been so.

The Italians are known for loving a festa or party, so the Comune organises regular events with the help of the amazing local musician (and my barber) Enrico, who tirelessly, and voluntarily, organises events in his capacity within the Borgo Alto, the local business community. You can regularly see him setting out chairs for musical concerts long before they start, and he is the last one tidying up at the end, when everyone has departed with a smile on their face. I am aware that there are a lot of people behind what goes on in Montaione, and I am still to meet many.

There are also many lovely cafés and *tabaccherie* in Montaione. Of particular note is the L'Antica Vineria, which translates in English to 'The Ancient Wine Shop' or, more naturally, 'The Old Wine Shop'. I have personally christened this *tabaccheria* the unofficial Montaione community centre. It is in the heart of the town and is filled with the buzz of conversation and laughter from the locals and tourists. Here you will find a busy, welcoming and well-stocked *tabaccheria.* They sell wonderful wines and delicious food in the town square, only a few metres from and looking onto the main town church, San Regolo, which dates back to 1369. I once spent an afternoon in L'Antica Vineria with my sister watching a wedding exiting this church. The following celebration was spectacular, with singing, dancing and cheering – 200 people were involved, from infants to the elderly, for about an hour. This was only the exit from the church service; the reception was held elsewhere. It's something my sister Lesley and I still often talk about. If you get a chance, please visit this *tabaccheria* and sit and people watch. Michel, Cristina and their wonderful staff will make you feel most welcome.

Montaione and the surrounding districts do have some expats, but not many. I have come across some non-Italians who have made their home here, and they talk about similar experiences to mine – wonderful place and people, difficult to pick up the language. One expat I've met and sometimes share a beer with is Steve, an Aussie. He moved here with his Italian wife and his beautiful family. He's a surfer and a lovely chap. I remember one evening enjoying a beer with him in the town square. When speaking with the Italians, I speak very slowly, or *piano-piano*, so that they can catch what I'm saying if they are not fluent in English. 'How … was … your … work … today?' On this particular evening, while enjoying Steve's company, he said, 'Barry, you do know my native tongue is English, don't you?' Out of habit, I had been speaking with Steve very slowly and exaggerating my words so that 'the listener' could understand. Sorry, Steve. We had a right laugh about that.

I've also become friends with a lovely expat Danish couple, Helle and Henning. They speak perfect English. In fact, Henning puts me to shame when I tell him I'm struggling with Italian. He can speak eight languages fluently – 'and a few others conversationally,' he says nonchalantly. I feel really small. They are wonderful company, and we enjoy a Friday night pizza together on occasion.

I also have to mention the wonderful Emma from Tutto Torna Antiques for making me feel super welcome. Originally from Edinburgh, she met an Italian and has been in Tuscany for nearly 40 years.

Like seemingly every town in the Western world, Montaione has been adversely affected by online shopping, COVID and economic struggles, but it still retains its beauty, resolve and optimism, and it is a sheer delight to be part of this outstanding community. Everything I have found so far in Montaione is truly wonderful, but its beauty to the eye would be nothing without the beauty of its people. The food, blue skies, weather, wine, outdoor living and landscapes are all amazing, but you can read about those from afar. It is the people that have made my transition to being an Italian resident a special journey of wonder, excitement and fulfilment. I thank them for that.

Chapter 30
A Life Full of Promise

As I sit here, reflecting on this extraordinary chapter of my life, it's impossible not to marvel at what has unfolded before me. From the stormy, wet and cold July promenade in Portrush, Northern Ireland, in 2023, to the sun-drenched hills of Tuscany, just a year later, my life has been a mix of adventure, uncertainty and discovery. Yet here I am, sipping an espresso, looking out at a landscape that feels like something straight out of a painting. And as I sit here, I can't help but think … wow, this is only the beginning.

When I first made the decision to leave behind the familiar shores of the north coast of Northern Ireland, I knew I was stepping into the unknown. I'd spent decades being a parent, a professional and, in many ways, a creature of habit. The empty nest, once looming as a source of melancholy, soon became a gateway to something far more exciting – a rebirth. My heart told me that Tuscany was the place where I could find a new rhythm, one that would allow me to embrace my passions and explore the quieter, more introspective side of my life and also of myself. And I had no idea just how rich and fulfilling it would be.

It wasn't easy, though. Let's not pretend that uprooting your life and moving to another country comes without its fair share of hurdles. The piles of paperwork, the baffling intricacies of Italian bureaucracy – it sometimes felt like I was in an endless game where the rules kept changing. There were moments of frustration, like when I thought I'd sorted everything for my healthcare registration only to be asked for a form I'd never heard of, when I had thirteen other documents in my hand. I laugh now but, at the time, I was a fish out of water, floundering through the language and the system clutching an abundance of laminated documents. But this was a small price to pay for what I was gaining.

Every challenge has taught me something. Whether it was figuring out how to navigate Italy's roads in a car held together by a prayer, learning to order coffee the right way or just grappling with the sheer beauty of everyday life here, I found myself growing. Tuscany has this way of getting under your skin. The people, with their warmth and generosity, welcomed me with open arms. They didn't care if my Italian was a mess. They saw me trying, and they appreciated it. In fact, those moments of awkwardness became stepping stones to friendships I now treasure.

And what friends they are. From the local workers who patiently smile when I order a bicycle of wine, to the fellow expats who have shared their own stories of trial and triumph, I've found myself surrounded by wonderful people. People who laugh with me, share in the beauty of this life and remind me that, even though I might be living alone, I am far from lonely. Solitude here isn't something to fear; it's a space in which I've found peace. I've been able to strip back the noise of modern life and reconnect with myself – something I think we all need to do.

It's not just the people who've made this experience special but also the place. Tuscany's hills, cypress trees and the golden light have a magic that feeds the soul. Every morning, as the sun rises and the warmth creeps into my bones, I'm reminded of why I've come here. Whether I'm strolling through the local markets, indulging in an afternoon gelato or simply sitting in the piazza watching the world go by, I feel a deep sense of contentment. It's a joy that comes from living in a place where beauty isn't confined to museums or galleries. It's everywhere – in every cobblestone, every olive tree, every moment. Yet, despite the peace I've found here, this is not a journey that ends in stillness. No, I'm just getting started. My adventures in Italy have been transformative, but now my sights are set on what's next. There are new businesses to launch, new ideas to explore and, yes, new mountains to climb, both literal and metaphorical.

I've already built the Toscana English Academy, and I'm proud of how far it's come, but that's just one part of the picture. The world is full of opportunities, and I've never felt more ready to seize them. There are new people to meet and new corners of this beautiful world to explore. The thing about adventure is, once you've tasted it, it's impossible to go back. The fire inside that led me here is burning bright, and I'm more determined than ever to keep feeding it.

For those who've followed my journey, I hope it's clear that this isn't just my story. It's a reminder to anyone reading this that it's never too late to reinvent yourself, to take that leap into the unknown and to live the life you've always dreamt of. Whether you're standing on a rainy promenade in Northern Ireland, contemplating your next step, or simply wondering if you have it in you to make a change, let me tell you, you do. Life is too short to settle for anything less than extraordinary. So here's to the future, to new adventures, to laughter and to living boldly. If you've been sitting on the sidelines, wondering whether it's time to make a change, I urge you, if it's right for you, go for it. There's a whole world out there, filled with intrigue, beauty and opportunities just waiting to be discovered. Follow your dreams and make your adventure happen – who knows, our paths may cross one day, on a road in Tuscany or at a café somewhere, sharing stories and raising a glass to an incredible life.

As for me? Well, this has been a memoir of my first 12 months since moving to Italy in August 2023, and you can bet there are many more chapters to be written, many more sunrises to greet and many more moments of joy and wonder ahead. Will this be my final move? I don't know. There are mountains yet to climb, dreams yet to chase, chapters yet to be written. It's a life still bursting with possibility …

… and I'm going to give it my all.

Printed in Dunstable, United Kingdom

64119586R00127